the message

A GUIDE TO BEING HUMAN · LD THOMPSON

Published by DIVINE ARTS
DivineArtsMedia.com

An imprint of Michael Wiese Productions
12400 Ventura Blvd. #1111
Studio City, CA 91604
(818) 379-8799, (818) 986-3408 (FAX)

Cover design by John Brenner
Copyediting by Annalisa Zox-Weaver
Book Layout by William Morosi
Printed by McNaughton & Gunn, Inc., Saline, Michigan

Manufactured in the United States of America

Library of Congress Cataloging-in-Publication Data

Thompson, L. D.
The message : a guide to being human / L.D. Thompson.
p. cm.
ISBN 978-1-61125-000-8
1. Spiritual life. 2. Spirit writings. I. Title.
BF1999.T516 2011
204.4--dc22

2011002826

Printed on Recycled Stock

Soul: \'sōl\ *noun*: the immaterial essence, animating principle, or actuating cause of an individual life.

CONTENTS

INTRODUCTION

This book is the result of years of listening. Years of study. Years of sharing what a benevolent teacher said about life and love and the heroic struggle to find joy and peace in the exquisite paradox of being human. The basic premise is this: Your life is designed by your Soul. The more you listen to your Soul and act upon its values and urgings, the more you realize that you are a spiritual being living in a body to fulfill a curriculum, and the more graceful and joyous your life becomes.

Many years ago, as I was leaving a grocery store in Los Angeles, my life changed forever. An East Indian man with long, black, oiled curls walked up to my car and said to me, "You have summoned me, and I've come to tell you of your life." I wondered if he was a recruiter for some cult. I wondered if he was dangerous. No one had ever said such a thing to me.

Then he began: "I know of the confusion and pain that you experience... the disappointment in the people you chose as your parents and the frustration that you know in your career. But know that your life is not about those distractions. There is a greater purpose for your existence. You are at a fork in the road. One path takes you to an early death and the other takes you to sublime fulfillment. As you are living now, there is great danger that you will choose the path that lays waste to the possibility for a greater understanding and delivers you to death's door without accomplishing your potential and what you came here to do."

We sat there for over two hours while he taught me the basic principles of how a person creates his or her life. He told me how repetitive thoughts, especially habitual thoughts of fear and desire, are ineffective in creating the life you want, and that only intentional, organized, and focused thought brings fulfillment. He talked about what I had come here to do, and how I could accomplish my goals if I could discipline my mind to think and feel that those goals had been realized — even if they really seemed out of my reach.

It was a lot to absorb, especially considering that I was on unemployment at the time and felt young and vulnerable in a very frightening world. Though I was trying to listen and understand, at one point I became completely overwhelmed and just couldn't hear him any more.

He then said to me, "Be at peace with me a moment."

He placed his right hand on his stomach just below his navel. His left hand was on his heart. And he said, "Focus there, in your body." Then his right hand moved to his navel "Now, there." I closed my eyes, and conscious thought abruptly stopped. There was no time, no sensation, really. Then he moved his hand to just below his sternum and let it rest there for an unknown amount of time. I did the same. Then to his heart, and to his throat, each time directing me to focus my mind there. Finally, he reached out and held my head with both of his hands. I was completely unprepared for what happened next. There were explosions of light in my head and rushes that felt like electricity up my spine. Just when I thought I couldn't take anymore, he let go of my head.

When I finally opened my eyes, I gazed on a world completely transformed. No more was the world a chaotic, senseless collection of disconnected images and events. It had become organized and rhythmic. It was still the parking lot of the grocery store, but as a woman opened her car door nearby and set her groceries inside, I could see how first there was thought — before there was her car or her children or her clothes or the groceries in the bag. Everywhere I looked, I saw the thought behind the reality.

The thing is, there was no pitch from this man. He didn't ask me to join a religion or to attend a seminar. He didn't ask me for money or demand any exchange for his time. His last words to me were, "You have a gift to give this world, and it comes from your Soul. Listen to it. Seek to know it. This that we have done opens the doors, that you might know."

And with that, I watched him walk away and literally vanish before my eyes.

His words were emblazoned in my mind. No one had ever spoken to me like that. No one had ever told me that I had a special gift or that I was here to fulfill a specific purpose. I furiously made notes. Somehow I had to hold on to what he had said. And, although I was transformed and giddy for days after that experience, life slowly bore down on me again and things seemed to return to normal.

But they never really did. After that night, when something was going wrong in my life, I no longer felt victimized. And, if I applied myself, I was able to trace everything back to a habitual pattern of thought.

Years later, I was living in Seattle when another extraordinary meeting took place.

I would go to a beach park at the end of each day, sit with my back against the same log, and welcome the gentle ebb and flow of the surf. My head would be bursting from the day, but the setting sun would soothe me and the wind would wash over me until my head was clear and quiet.

One evening when I had settled in, a rush of soundless sound filled my head — what you hear when you are somewhere truly quiet. The only sounds were the sea and the wind moving through the tall beach grass. Then I heard a voice in my head, as clear as if someone outside of me had spoken: "I am Solano. I have been with you throughout time and have awaited this moment. This moment is the result of much preparation.

"I have come to guide you, not to coddle you. The first and greatest lesson that you are learning is that you are free. You are free to choose. You can choose to live a life that is prescribed by society, or you can choose to break the form and know more of yourself than is ordinarily known.

"The most important thing for you to understand is that you know. Know that you know all things. Be audacious, and instead of waiting for knowledge or waiting to be told, know. Feel your life, your substance. All knowledge that you desire is contained in that. When you meet other people, before they even speak, you contact their essence. In that moment you receive everything about them, all knowledge, every thought and action, past and future. It is for convenience in your society that you are taught not to know. It is also from fear. People fear to know one another. They fear intimacy. They fear that if they knew, really knew another person, they would be disillusioned. And it is true, they would be dis-illusioned in the truest sense of that word. Nearly everyone carries some shame. The lens of knowing is one that reflects that pain. If you see another being clearly, then you must see yourself clearly. If you see other beings intimately, what they show you will reveal yourself to you. If you are to see others clearly, you must fearlessly look at yourself, forgive your limitations, and acknowledge your exquisite uniqueness.

"You are now ready. You have been calling for this change in your life. You desire to be able to help others. If you are to help others, then you must will yourself to see what you have not been encouraged to see, hear what you have not been taught to hear: the thoughts behind the words. To be a knower is to look upon another and really see. Their face, their body, the light that emanates from them. These things tell you what their mask would hide. Listen to them; behind their words is the story of their lives, their hopes and dreams, and their hidden shames. But you must listen.

"That is all for now. We will speak again. In the days to come you will begin to realize that your Soul is the seat of sentience within you. That sentience is on a path, a trajectory, if you will, and the more you study your life, the more the Soul's design will be revealed. You are here to fulfill that design. You are here to study that curriculum. When you shift your perspective to see your life as your Soul sees it — the fulfillment of its curriculum — all things in your life take on new meaning. When that shift in perspective comes, you will be carried forward on a tide of Divine inspiration. I am with you now and always. Be at peace."

Being skeptical — I grew up in a very traditional Christian home and rejected religion early on due to what, in my experience, seemed like rampant hypocrisy — I wasn't about to take such an experience on faith. What I couldn't ignore, however, was how moving it was to hear such empowering words. Those words compelled me to test this source, this voice, to see what value it had in my life.

In the months that followed, I left the city, left my career, and truly let go of preconceived notions about what my life was supposed to be. Like a dandelion seed on the wind, I let myself be picked up and carried while I studied my life, my emotions, and my desires. In instance after instance, when I turned within and listened, I was guided surely and supported completely. When I resisted and judged a situation, I stumbled. So I began to trust Solano. Over and over again, I found that what he told me was right and guided me to greater understanding and greater freedom and providence.

Since that evening, I have been able to hear his voice whenever I open myself to it.

Many people have benefited from the wisdom that comes from Solano. Bodies and hearts have been healed, people have been helped during their passing, children have been guided, and careers have been launched, but most of all this benevolent teacher has taught people that everything in their lives happens by the design of their Soul.

This book is like a book of hours. You can refer to it in the course of a day, and receive guidance about how to view your life and what your Soul is striving to teach you.

To make a distinction for the reader between my voice and my thoughts and the voice and thoughts of Solano, the latter is represented in standard font.

We've all matriculated; that is to say, we're here on Earth, and Earth is nothing but a great big university where we may learn every noble virtue imaginable. But many of us get caught up in the struggle for survival and success, and forget that we're really struggling to learn, to become better, to become more Divine.

The path to this wisdom is through the Soul — something each of us comes equipped with. Each Soul is the doorway through which we may access the Source of knowledge, wisdom, compassion, strength, courage, and love — simply, God.

THE COMMITMENTS

You are here to learn what it is to be wholly and completely One with the Source of all.

— *Solano*

You are experiencing the human state of consciousness for a good reason: to learn to be one with God, the Source of all that is. You place yourself in this state of consciousness to have experiences that fulfill your Soul's aim. Experiences that — once you move beyond this state of consciousness — will give you the ability to express yourself as you wish. The goal here is to help you determine what your Soul's curriculum is. Once you discover that, you will have guidelines upon which to base all of your decisions.

Understanding why you are here in a body to begin with provides guidelines for facing conflicting emotions. Such emotions then become intriguing rather than a source of anxiety. This realization allows a deeper commitment to your Soul's curriculum. There are moments when you will question the value of your life, and question whether being fully engaged in your life is what you truly desire. Deepening into life requires having a set of personal guidelines that, when followed, enable you to be fully present in your life. Being present affords access to all knowledge, all power, indeed, to enlightenment itself.

As you go about your life, negative patterns or situations may present themselves over and over again. These negative patterns can prevent you from feeling well centered. In such moments, you have choices to make. But what do you base your choices on? How do you move, how do you act? Do you defend yourself, embody righteous anger, or is it best simply to be loving and forgiving? How do you decide whether to be aggressive and ambitious or simply to attempt to avoid confrontation? These sorts of questions come up.

To overcome repeating negative patterns requires a set of commitments on your part.

CHANGE

When you commit to change, you begin to recognize that change is going to occur whether you consciously agree with it or not.

— *Solano*

Change is inevitable. Change fuels your life. Inertia is antilife. Change is what life is built upon. You are like a magnet. Do you remember the experiment where you put a magnet under a piece of paper with sprinkled metal filings over it? The filings arrange themselves in a pattern that reveals the invisible electromagnetic field of the magnet. The pattern provides an excellent illustration of what it is like for a Soul dwelling on Earth.

When you do the experiment, you cannot see the magnetic field, but you can see its effect. You are very much like that. You can see your effect in the world, but you do not always see your field of energy. The field of energy grows and changes from moment to moment. Your field changes because you collect new experiences, new wisdom. You incorporate that wisdom, and it contributes to your magnetic field. You are not a fixed reality. Your body, which you think of as somewhat solid, changes very slowly, so you look at it as a fixed thing. This permanence is a complete illusion.

Many people are able to accept this notion intellectually. But you must take that knowledge and drive it deeply into your body, so that every moment of every day, every opportunity for consciousness, you hold the thought that you are energy first. You are consciousness first.

You are more like a whirlwind than like a tree or a rock. A human being is a confluence, a convergence of energies. Your energy field creates what you relate to as your physical body. Yet, your body is as mutable and changeable as a whirlwind. When you consider a whirlwind, you do not think of it as a fixed thing. It is always in motion. So are you, constantly. Science has identified that in the human body, within each cell, somewhere on the order of six trillion things are going on in any given moment. If six

trillion things are occurring within each cell, that cell is in motion — a phenomenal amount of motion.

You need only think of a car in order to understand that it is easier to steer when you are in motion than when you are standing still. Trying to turn a car that is moving very slowly is extremely arduous, as you know from parking. But if that same vehicle has just a bit of momentum, you can gracefully move it where you want. So it is when you recognize that you are in motion and not fixed in your consciousness. When you understand that you are not fixed in your particular patterns of emotion, when you understand that you are not fixed in the particular patterns of manifestation in your body — aging, disease, addictions, and so on — you have the ability to adjust and move your direction with grace. You can then manifest with ease the inevitable change in your life.

The altered ego, as you well know, sometimes finds itself fixating on a moment, on a situation, on a particular event, trying to hold on to that moment for as long as possible. That action is anti-life. Resisting change does not support your commitment to life. The more you cling to a given circumstance, solution, or relationship, the more the Soul marches on without your conscious agreement because you are too busy clinging to a skeleton that is turning to dust in your arms. Rather than clinging, let yourself accept that change is occurring and that change is inevitable. Doing so directs your attention to the motion you are in, and allows you to be more effective at steering to where you want to go.

This first commitment — change — was one of the hardest for me. Not theoretically, of course. I could get my arms around the theory that everything changes. But then I would find myself in a relationship, and when change occurred and the two of us would move in different directions, I would resist that change with all my might. Or a loved one would take ill, and I would realize that he or she was dying, and I would do all in my power to resist that change. Or I, myself, would experience a health crisis or some other challenging passage in my life, and I would find myself resisting the changes.

Part of the difficulty in change is that it stirs deep and sometimes challenging emotions: fear, sadness, grief, anger, jealousy, longing. And, being human, we are compelled by our emotions, often letting them determine our thoughts and our behavior.

Here's what I've come to understand: Emotions are the tools with which our Souls communicate to us and move us. When my life calls for profound change, my emotions speak to me of my fears but also of my hopes and dreams. When I went through the break-up of a long-term relationship, I was plunged into profound fear, insecurity, grief, and despair. I spent many months trying to avoid, transform, understand, somehow manipulate those emotions. Ultimately, I realized that my Soul had called me to one of life's most difficult lessons: learning that the source of my well-being is my relationship to myself, not my relationship to another (or to money or sex or drugs or recognition, or any of the other things we humans come to think of as the source of well-being).

Once I realized that my emotions were an important level of communication about the change I was undergoing — but not the change itself — then I was able to embrace their message (concern for the well-being of the body and personality), relinquish my fixation on them, and drop down into the place where the change was taking place — on the level of the Soul. Then I discovered that the Soul was directing me to a deeper relationship with myself, the spark of foreverness that is my true self.

From that place of deeper understanding, I was able to become a witness to my emotions — not to fixate on them but rather to understand that, as the etymology of the word indicates, they are in motion. Not identifying with them, I allowed them to change.

KNOWING

Knowing is a matter of remembering every moment that you are the Divine Intelligence.

— *Solano*

Knowing — individuals are often most insistent upon denying it, because inhabiting knowingness causes you to give up any claim to being a victim. However, you actually do know the person you are falling in love with. You know your compatibility with a given career or job. You know what it will take to heal your heart or a physical wound. You know what it takes to overcome an addiction. You know where you should live and how to deal with your family. You know, you know, you know.

When you live your life acknowledging that you *know*, acknowledging that you make choices sometimes *despite* knowing, you can never be victimized. You are then a sentient being, consciously choosing your actions. The Soul works with whatever choices you make, and you have the ability to make choices based on conscious knowing.

When you commit to knowing, you commit to remembering that everything is intelligence — that you are intelligence dwelling in an ocean of intelligence. All that intelligence is conversing with itself in every moment.

Because you are that intelligence, because you are built of intelligence, only your willfulness keeps you in ignorance. You know why you are here; you know how to access your deepest intuition. You tell yourself that if you truly did know, then you would not have fallen down or chosen that rotten relationship or gotten fired.

Forget what you think *knowingness* is. Knowing comes from being fully present in your body, in your life. Knowing acknowledges that you are in the hands of your Soul's infinite wisdom. When you use your mind to try to figure out your life or a situation, you actually prevent knowingness.

Conscious knowingness is accessed by the first commitment: change. When you commit to change, you commit to living in the moment, to being seated in the moment. Knowingness does not come from examining your past or anticipating your future. Both past and future are contained in this moment, in the present. The present is where knowingness dwells.

You may be thinking, "Just saying the words does not make it easier to access knowingness." That is true. It requires, first, being resolute that there is nothing you fear to know. Secondly, you accept that all knowledge is born of the essential energy of the universe. And you are born of that. Do you know, for instance, how to divide a cell or digest an apple or grow a human baby? Would you be able to articulate the critical path for those actions without missing a step here or there? Yet you are capable of these things, and more. You engage in such activities constantly because you *know* how to in your deepest intelligence.

But what about the really thorny questions? "What is my purpose?" or "How do I find a perfect mate?" or "What happens when I die?" Too often you let an apparent lack of understanding or accomplishment influence your belief about your ability to know. Such questions make it even more important that you embrace the knowingness of the Soul. Your Soul, the essence of who you are, knows why you are here. It is driving you toward the fulfillment of your existence in every moment, with or without your conscious cooperation. Your Soul knows whether being in a relationship or being rich or poor or being creatively fulfilled or searching for fulfillment — at this particular moment — is part of the curriculum. When you dwell in your body and inhabit the Soul's perspective of foreverness, all knowledge is available to you.

Now is a time of great transition here on Earth. During this time of transition, your commitment to knowing is even more urgent. You must be tireless in your demand upon yourself to see from a deeper perspective. The Soul's eyes see everything in order in the universe, in the collective consciousness, and in your individual life. When you demand such knowing of yourself, you do not fixate on how things should be or how bad the economy is or how the prevailing political climate is affecting the world.

When you commit to knowing, you commit to understanding that everything in your life appears before you as answered prayers. The same is true in the larger context. The collective consciousness functions just as your individual consciousness functions; it has a tone, a frequency that dictates what is magnetized to it. As communication increases, more conscious beings function as a sort of societal Soul that possesses the ability to bring its values to bear on the larger body, the collective consciousness. The aim, then, of those who are more conscious is to evoke the Soul's values in the collective consciousness by embodying those values in their individual lives. To accomplish this aim requires a commitment to knowing.

The greatest inhibitor to knowing is plain and simple: blatant disregard of what you know to be right for you and for your growth.

There was a time in my life when I felt very lost. I was deeply troubled by what seemed like an insoluble conundrum. I was in a relationship that was very important to me, yet being in it was making me lose energy, lose my sense of self. I kept praying and meditating for an answer, and despite what I felt in my heart and experienced in my dreams, I kept choosing the relationship.

I am reminded of the story of a man who was stranded in a house while the river was rising, and he prayed for God to save him. The police were going door to door, warning everyone to evacuate because of the danger from the river. They got to the man's door and he turned them away, saying, "GOD will save me." As the water rose, the man climbed to the second floor. Some people came with a boat and offered to rescue him, but he declined again, saying, "GOD will save me." As the water continued to rise, he wound up on the roof of the house. Some people in a helicopter came by and tried to save him but, you guessed it, he declined the offer, saying, "GOD will save me!" So he drowned and went to Heaven, and in a fit of anger asked God, "Why didn't you save me?" And God said, "I sent you the police, a boat, and a helicopter. Why did you stay in the house?"

I was acting like the man in the house. I wanted the Heavens to part, for some miraculous force to reach down and pluck me from my troubled waters. Ultimately, I realized that it was my responsibility to acknowledge the guidance I was receiving from within, and to act upon it. When I did — when I called a halt to the relationship as it was — it took many moments of being steadfast and congruent about the choice, the decision to act allowed me to come home to myself, to embrace my Soul's curriculum, and to engage in the growth my Soul intended for me.

Knowing requires both acknowledgment and action.

INTUITION

Intuition is the native ability of the Soul.

— *Solano*

Your most direct means of communication with your Soul takes place through your intuition. The commitment to intuition requires living your life identifying with your Soul. Once you understand your intuitive capacity and know how to access it, you begin to follow the curriculum of your Soul rather than simply reacting to what happens to you.

Much of what is said about accessing intuition focuses rather narrowly on the pineal gland (the third eye) and the pituitary gland (the crown chakra). These glands are, indeed, important parts of the intuitive process, but there is more to it, as we shall see. The pineal gland is intricately involved with the optic nerve; it has the specific function of translating subtle vibrations in

Chakras are energy centres along the spine located at major branches of the human nervous system. Chakras are considered to be a point or nexus of biophysical energy of the human body. They are the basic component of your energy field.

your energy field into an internal vision.

The pituitary gland's function is to take your current level of knowledge and translate it into matter. It is responsible for transforming your very body. Every seven years your body is brand new on the cellular level. The pituitary places what you know into each cell. The cells that are being replaced this very minute contain whatever knowledge you have fully embraced.

More fundamentally, however, intuition is a matter of understanding your Soul's relationship to your heart. The heart will tell you everything you need to know about how to live. You can access this knowledge through a simple test: Does my heart feel open, or does it feel contracted? If you apply that question to every situation, consistently choosing the feeling of openness, your *vibratory frequency* will lift such that you begin to live life guided by your intuition.

The vibratory frequency of a human body is measurable. It is eight to ten times faster than the electrical frequency of the biological current of the physical body. Your vibratory frequency is the magnetic resonance that envelops you. It raises and lowers depending on mood, health, drug and food consumption, and habitual thought patterns.

When your heart contracts, you move into a state, an emotion, a response, a frequency that closes you off from your intuition. When your heart opens, you move into a Soul-identified life. This openness provides you with a single test for absolutely every decision you must make. When you open your heart to the things you fear, you open yourself to your Soul's wisdom and challenge your ability to remain in a loving frame of mind.

When you are open to the things you fear, wisdom can move through your body and be translated by the pineal gland as vision and by the pituitary gland as knowledge. This response, in turn, transforms the body on a cellular level. For some, the adrenal glands provide what is called a *gut feeling*, a kinesthetic response to what the Soul already knows.

Gut feeling: a visceral physical response to an intuitive impression.

Leading with your heart releases life energy — Love — into the dense frequency of the collective consciousness. This phenomenon is quite different from an energy leakage. Leaking energy is the result of fear or unconscious addictive choices that sap energy from your field. Releasing life energy, on the contrary, is the result of consciously acting from the Soul's impulse. Moving with intuition as your lead — not leading with your intellect but leading with your heart — releases life energy.

One candle can light an entire room and allow what is not visible to be seen. More candles in that same room allow more detail, more knowledge, more wisdom, more navigability. As you access your intuition by dropping down into your Soul, you release life energy and Love into your world. Such a release transforms the Earth, allowing you to dwell where you can see more, where you can understand more, where you can express more joy.

In terms of intuition, the body is a nanosecond behind the Soul. The Soul knows all, in every moment. As you train yourself to drop into your Soul, to access its knowledge about your life, many times in the course of the day, you will find that intuition has become commonplace for you.

Even when you become adept at accessing your intuition, the intellect will remain a powerful force in your life, because of the culture you live in. The world pays great homage to information. Information instantly engages the linear mind, the intellect. The intellect is in the domain of the *altered ego* — the aspect of your self that takes on the values and judgments of your society, family, and tribe, and imposes them critically, and usually inconsistently, upon you.

Altered ego: the aspect of one's personality that responds to criticism and shaming; a defensive part of the persona. personality

When you begin your day, whether at home with your computer and telephone or in the marketplace, you engage a frequency that is equivalent to the linear mind, the intellect. This culture believes that information is power. The good news is that a great many people now have access to information and to the power it holds. What has suffered, however, is personal quietude, a calm understanding of life — Soulfulness.

In practicing this new communication with your Soul, notice when you find yourself relying on your intellect. When you recognize this impulse, simply draw yourself down into your heart, as though your eyes and ears were there. Let your senses center in your Soul and then look out at your world, at your creative reality. Examine what the mind talks about: your fears, your anxieties, your hopes, your ambitions, your pains, your frailties. Then drop into your Soul and examine the mind's conversations from the Soul's perspective. The Soul has a different perspective than the intellect. The Soul's perspective is infused with enthusiasm and fearlessness and an exquisite Love of self.

Let your Soul's enthusiasm release life-energy by opening your heart to your life. Let it be in communication with your surroundings. In this way, you make a commitment to intuition so you may move *with* your Soul's curriculum

NONJUDGMENT

You operate in every moment from your greatest accumulation of knowledge.

— *Solano*

Think about how often you judge yourself. Judging yourself is tantamount to judging creation. Judging yourself is like taking the most cherished of innocent creatures and damning it for being what it is. Everyone is an innocent — precious and pure. You are utterly and completely without blame in all things.

Now, we're not talking about responsibility; you *are* responsible for your life. Blame is different from responsibility because the tone of judgment accompanies blame. The altered ego considers your age, your experience — all the knowledge you have collected — and often concludes that somehow you should know better. And so you judge yourself, thinking you should be doing better, should be further along, should be more successful, blaming yourself for not doing better.

Judgment is discernment gone awry. It is closed-mindedness. Sometimes a person comes to a decision point about her life, an individual, a place, or any given life dynamic, and that decision becomes a default thought process, a habitual response. At this point, judgment is no longer a conscious thought process. This is the way the smaller mind (not the Universal Mind) takes a shortcut. The small mind says, "I know that thing. I know what that means. I know what it is, and I know what I have determined about it."

Judgment is equated with closed-mindedness because in judgment the mind becomes a closed system, a system in which the same pathways are walked every time. Judgment is erroneously thought of as a way to conserve energy. Yet no energy is actually conserved through judgment.

For example, you walk through the grocery store and see someone you know, someone you have judged negatively in past interactions. Your altered ego believes it is conserving energy by judging because now you don't have to let that person in. Their light field — the field of energy that surrounds their body — is rebuffed; you exclude them by judgment so you don't need to comingle frequencies.

Your judgment, however, is the very hook into their light field and their frequency. Judgment links you right in with them. In that moment energy is expended. Judgment requires greater energy than the energy of a blessing.

A blessing acknowledges your Soul and the other person's Soul: One Soul witnessing another Soul striving to make sense of what she is viewing through her own kaleidoscopic lens. Her particular lens is filled with bits of glass of different colors than yours, but that is what her Soul has called her to. Falling into a habit of judging is easy when your life is surrounded by more people than animals, fields, trees, brooks, or mountains.

Confronted with so many people, the altered ego goes into overdrive. It desires to keep you safe, and therefore closes off access to your deeper, more Soulful self by deeming things inappropriate, not desirable, or even worse. Watching television, seeing everything going on in the world, often leads the small mind to judgement and fear. When you engage this response, you connect yourself to the very energy and dynamics you judge. Far better in such moments is to bless all the Souls and events you witness. Realizing that all people are being called to their curriculum by their Soul will help you remember that everything happens for growth — individual and collective.

Removing judgment and cultivating engaged detachment — the state where you are fully present and grounded in your body and, at the same time, identify yourself as a spiritual being — are the means by which you can confront things that your mind would rather not contemplate. Engaged detachment allows you to understand the situations, people, and emotions that manifest in your life.

With an attitude of engaged detachment, the mind can go about its business of being creative. When you notice your thoughts dwelling on negativity or judgment is precisely the moment you should actively place your thoughts on something more expansive. You can prevent yourself from habitually defaulting to those thoughts.

If you find yourself getting up every day and having the same inner dialogue that you had the day before, about the very same issue, what do you accomplish? This habit generates an energy pattern in the magnetic field around your body, reaffirming your habitual experience over and over again.

You are precisely who you are supposed to be in this moment, but your altered ego judges where you are, and what you have achieved or not achieved. Bringing the altered ego into alignment with the Soul's curriculum is a matter of relinquishing judgment. Relinquishing judgment about your own life has an ancillary benefit: relinquishing judgment of others. Nonjudgment avows that all are innocent in their Souls. When the altered ego recognizes this innocence, a complete alignment of intellect, personality, and Soul will allow the vibratory frequency of your body to lift.

If you were able to see yourself in this moment through the eyes of the Soul, you would see a pattern of light, not the density of your body. When you relinquish judgment of yourself and others, the vibratory frequency of your light field lifts and you become lighter, as seen through the Soul's eyes.

When you become lighter, your frequency moves faster, and you are able to move with greater grace and empowerment. Your magnetism is more compelling, and the physical world around you organizes itself to match the highest octave of what you imagine your experience to be, as a unique, individuated consciousness.

Committing to life is committing to change, committing to knowingness and intuition. It is the suspension of judgment. It is bringing the altered ego into alignment with what you are in your essence: pure, innocent consciousness. Ultimately, this process guides you to the knowledge, fully embodied, that you are Divine.

The moment when the boundaries between you and other people and nature begin to blur, you find yourself in a cognizant, intelligent, and interconnected universe.

Relinquishing judgment is tricky for me because judgment of myself and others is how I try to avoid change. Particularly, I notice that I judge those with whom I am most intimate, wishing they would do certain things and not do other things. But if I direct those desires for someone else to change to my own life, then I am able to identify the ways in which I am trying to avoid changing my own attitudes and behavior.

When I relinquish the judgment and stop projecting judgment onto others (I wish you would grow up, be more patient, be more open-minded, stop being critical, stop being indiscriminate, start being more productive, be more flexible, etc.), I suddenly find myself seated in the power to make positive, thorough, and lasting change within myself.

FEARLESSNESS

Realizing that every situation you find yourself in is there to serve your Soul's curriculum is the most potent antidote to fear.

— *Solano*

If the very first thing you do as you confront any situation or thought or addiction is demand fearlessness of yourself, you will be able to approach each situation with complete presence of mind.

How does one embody fearlessness? What does it take?

Name anything. The most heinous of tragedies, the most awesome of opportunities, the most grievous of losses, a personal blow, like disease — all of these circumstances are there to serve you. They come at your beck and call.

You may wonder how you could have called for an unpleasant experience. Remember that the commitment to knowing means understanding that your Soul has brought you to this moment. It has brought you to this unique blend of patterns in which you find yourself for the purpose of fulfilling your Soul's curriculum. Your Soul's purpose is to educate you in the knowledge that you are Divine.

Your Soul is moving you along the journey of individual expression so that you may experience yourself as an intelligence that is part of the great ocean of intelligence. Thus, recognizing every event as the answer to prayer allows you to move out of fear and into courage.

All too often you experience fear and don't know what to do about it. Perhaps you are skilled enough to trace an anxiety to its source. Perhaps the source is your bank account or your relationship or your health or your job or your career. Perhaps you feel that your life is falling short of what you expected.

It is very easy for you to dwell in fear. Perhaps you are addicted to overeating, and when you experience fear you head for the cupboard. Perhaps your addiction of choice is television, so you turn it on. Or maybe it is sex, and you manipulate circumstances so you can forget yourself at the moment of orgasm. Perhaps you are addicted to a sense-dulling drug.

Fear may cause you to cling to your youth, but clinging to youth is the result of erroneous thinking; behind that clinging is the expectation that you can cling to life. You can no more cling to this life than you can cling to a whirlwind. It whirls, it picks up what it picks up, and it throws off what it throws off. It is a thing of beauty. It is a thing of dynamism.

Embrace the knowledge that you are vital because you are committed to life. Embrace the knowledge that you are a dynamic force because you are God Divine. In so doing, you affirm that everything that comes into your life serves the process of change. It serves the process of continuing your motion, allowing you to be a force of nature.

Addictions are signposts of your fears. They are attempts to avoid what you fear. The moment an addiction arises is the moment you pay attention. Do not medicate, do not pull yourself away from the fear by deadening it or distracting yourself from it. Look at it; look at the fear and name it *providence*. Call it an answered prayer.

What does this response accomplish? It allows you to be in motion and aware of your motion, aware that you are changing. Fearlessness — which means labeling all things in your life *opportunity* — is proactive positivism, the embrace of an optimistic view of life. Optimism is the only view of life that is sound, because optimism recognizes that you exist forever as a life force, and that you are forever being served.

Proactive positivism is the act of looking at all the things in your life that you feel negative about or that cause you fear, and imprinting on them the understanding that everything happens in order to move you forward. Everything happens for you to achieve the goal of lifting your vibratory frequency. The higher your vibratory frequency, the more you inhabit the realm of grace that comes from understanding that you are Divine.

I found myself in a situation in which I was afraid to make a decision as to how to confront a project partner about a miscommunication we'd had. The root cause was fear of loss of love (or approval). I considered her to be someone of value, and there was much promise in the relationship going forward.

I thought about many different ways of dealing with the situation, including ignoring it, taking all the responsibility for the miscommunication, or building a case to defend myself and counter her case. Finally, I realized that I needed most of all to step into fearlessness and respond from a deeply centered, loving, but truthful and open place.

The result was not miraculous. There wasn't suddenly a choir from Heaven proclaiming that I had passed the test, but I was able to overcome what seemed to be a paralysis of expression by remembering this simple yet powerful commitment. I expressed my perspective on the situation without blaming her, accepting my role and responsibility in the situation. The communication didn't ultimately change her attitude or position about the miscommunication, but I felt balanced, complete, and open to ongoing dialogue, and months later, we were able to take the relationship up again stronger than ever.

OPENNESS

There are no secrets.

— *Solano*

Most people believe it is possible to keep secrets, but there really is no such thing as a secret. All that you are is apparent. It is apparent in the residue of your life. In other words, you do not live in a vacuum. You do not dwell separately from anything.

All is known. Committing to live your life openly is life-affirming. When you live openly, all your peccadilloes, all your neuroses, and all your shames are understood as the mere judgments of your altered ego.

When you are closed, you affirm that there is something about you that is not integrated into the fabric of what God is — and there is no such thing. Every part of you, every deed, every word you have ever spoken, every way in which you have ever disappointed yourself or, rather, disappointed your altered ego, every way in which you have ever felt ashamed — those are all a part of the fabric of God. Living in this knowledge engenders openness.

Every day, find ways of living more openly. Engage people that you otherwise would not. Engage them knowing that the moment they contact you, they know who you are. The moment you contact them, you know them.

The intellect and the altered ego will say this is not true. You are constantly convincing yourself that you do not know (and that others do not know). But the Soul knows all, in every moment. When you allow yourself to hold that thought, you begin to realize how much knowledge is available to you just by dropping down into your Soul's innate wisdom. Next time you have a meeting with someone you have never met before, for example, reflect on it beforehand — not with your mind, but with your Soul. You will be amazed at how much comes to you, which will then be confirmed.

The more you make a path to that place within where you are simple *is-ness*, the more you begin to discover that you have as much right to *be* as anyone else. You have as much right to express yourself as anyone else. With that knowledge, living openly, unafraid of expressing yourself becomes easier.

There's a Janis Joplin song lyric that goes, "Freedom's just another word for nothing left to lose." It's like that with people who are unafraid to be who they are. They are frequently larger than life because they aren't ashamed of who they are, who they love; they're unafraid of what others think about their accomplishments, or lack thereof. These are the people I think of as authentic. *It's as if they realized they have every right to be who they are, and just started being completely open about it. As a result, their energy field became larger than life.*

Have you ever seen a naked person among a crowd of clothed people? The clothed people usually have very strong reactions. They are afraid of the naked person, or at least uneasy, despite the inherent vulnerability in nakedness. It's an excellent metaphor for this commitment. Openness is like nakedness: There is power in it. Nothing left to lose.

GRATITUDE

Gratitude grows out of the understanding that life is forever and profoundly providential.

— *Solano*

The commitment to gratitude for your life, your struggles, your gifts, your foreverness — gratitude for every experience you have ever had — changes your experience of your own life more than anything else. You cannot sincerely offer gratitude without openness in your heart. It is impossible. When you consistently choose a feeling of openness, your vibratory frequency lifts and you begin to live life directed by your intuition.

When you let go of what *should be* and embrace fully and gratefully *what is*, you find yourself in motion in your life. This change allows you to continually lift your vibratory frequency such that you rise up to a state of grace: the state in which synchronicity and a life marked by providence become your prevailing experience.

I counseled a young man who had a very traumatic experience when he was in high school. He had been the popular kid in school, active in sports, choir, and drama. He came from a good family, had lots of friends, and was well liked by students and teachers alike. Then he made what he thought to be the biggest mistake of his life: He fell in love with another boy. In reality, he didn't consider that the mistake; the mistake was that he told a friend, in confidence, about his feelings for the boy. The friend told another friend, and in one day this golden boy went from the most popular kid in school to taking the brunt of brutal rumors, slurs, and hazing.

He held the belief that this event was the moment his life had irrevocably changed from one of a privileged insider to that of disgraced pariah. He had struggled with this sense of loss and betrayal for years. Most of all, he struggled with the sense of having made a really stupid mistake that cost him dearly.

Our work was in constantly asking what there was to be grateful for in this situation — how his Soul's curriculum had been served. For a long time, all he was able to manage was that having been knocked down had made him more compassionate and caring. Being laid low had made him stronger and more resilient. It made him a better friend to those who befriended him despite his disgrace.

But it was a long time before he was able to feel genuine gratitude toward his betrayer, let alone gratitude for his betrayal of himself.

Gratitude, when it finally came, was a result of his understanding that he had not made a mistake, but that he had, in fact, taken a risk: the risk of being open, the risk of being seen. From there, he was able to embrace with gratitude that the event had set him on a path, and instead of feeling it was a path of shame and disgrace, he was able to embrace with gratitude the gifts that were his as a result of that fateful time in his life.

When feeling grateful is a challenge, practice engaged detachment. Being engaged but detached allows you to adopt a more expansive perspective. It requires shifting your viewpoint to understand your life as a kaleidoscope of experiences that move and change. The faces and careers and relationships that make up your life — those are the patterns. They shift and change. They are all of the same fabric, and you are the constant.

You are the I that views it all and — at the same moment — is engaged in it. That I is indestructible and forever.

Yet, detachment alone is not enough.

Be grateful for your existence and for the wisdom that you are gathering. All the changes you put yourself through allow you to embrace engaged detachment. You realize that the kaleidoscopic images you are looking at will change. And change again. All of it changes. You are, in your Soul, the only constant.

In that constancy, being grateful prevents you from trying to grab at the bits of colored kaleidoscope glass as they tumble. Instead, you simply allow the picture to move and change, appreciating its colors. Gratitude works with every situation you face, addressing the mind, the altered ego, the body, and the Soul.

Every moment, your thoughts, your actions, and the frequency you generate reverberate out into mutable, changeable, plastic reality. Then they reverberate back into your life as the condensation of your experiences.

Often the mind uses this condensation as proof that you are not worthy, or that you have lived poorly, or that you should be ashamed, or that you are behind in your progress. It is vital that you detach yourself from those judgments.

Your particular frequency reverberates out into this plastic reality and comes back as a signal, as a sign — but also as a gift to you: not as punishment, or because you deserve a hard lesson. None of that is true. Your frequency reverberates back to your existence innocently, purely, as a means of teaching. In this way, you provide yourself with your own teaching tools.

If a situation reverberates back into your life and you are not happy with it, you are likely to search for the cause, a thought or a moment that you can judge as a mistake. It is crucial to remove judgment from such moments. Removing judgment will assure that you can continue to move and not get hung up on that specific lesson's reflection. Just as the kaleidoscope turns, the scenes that appear before you turn and then they give way. It is all plastic and responsive. The phrase "It is God's good pleasure to give to you the kingdom" applies in every moment, to everything that comes into your life, whether you think of it as difficult or grace-filled. Everything is a gift given by a conscious, intelligent Source — not a cause for judgment.

Committing to gratitude allows you to appreciate and passionately embrace everything in your life.

THE CURRICULUM

Your Soul is responsible for your growth. It establishes the curriculum that you adhere to in your life.

— *Solano*

You have never made a mistake in your life, not one. You have not stumbled or erred even once. Every moment you are presented with opportunities to remember who you are, and those opportunities come from your Soul. You may experience things that are horrendous, painful, abusive, and frightening. Even those experiences are part of your Soul's curriculum.

You are constantly growing into the responsibility that accompanies knowing fully that you are God. If you suddenly understood that you are God and could destroy worlds and create entirely new ones with a simple thought, would you be responsible enough not to succumb to the temptations inherent in such power?

It is in the best interest of all creation for you to be so empowered. God, the Source of all that is, wants you to use your prodigious creativity and to inhabit your innate power — the power of creation.

God is the life force that allows anything to be. Why would God allow anything negative or violent or hurtful or diminishing or humiliating? The answer is very simple: Every being experiences some form of addictive behavior or compelling fear, which he or she is drawn to over and over again. Such instances have been agreed upon by the Soul. The Soul creates these experiences so that the individual has the opportunity to meet and overcome fear. Being pulled from your center by such an experience is a signpost. It points to a circumstance in which you do not know yourself to be one with the benevolent, abundant, compassionate intelligence that governs all creation.

The transformation of such ignorance into knowing is the basis of the Soul's curriculum.

Where you are vulnerable to addiction, or to fear is
where you have the ability to gain your greatest power.

— *Solano*

When one is consciously on the path of spiritual evolution, the path that leads to the power to create at will, temptations arise. To be clear: Temptation is not merely being tempted to do something that is illicit or hedonistic. Sometimes the temptation to be fearful or angry is the greatest draw in one's life. Such temptations arise repeatedly so that you might deepen, you might grow more still, you might relinquish the reactions that come from your genetics, from your childhood, and from attitudes you have come to identify as your self.

The Soul calls these necessary temptations into your life so you can unhook from these attitudes and behaviors. It calls into vivid display any values that are not the Soul's values, but rather are the values that have been embraced by the personality and the altered ego. It draws them forth so that they may be transformed.

Identify your addictions and your fears. This is the first step to reclaiming your greatest potential power.

— *Solano*

Consider the addiction to approval. The approval seeker is convinced that if he can find enough approval, he will be safe. He constantly tries to be appropriate, seeking others who fit into his altered ego's desire for approval (or disapproval). The desire for approval is the desire for security. One who is addicted to approval feels unsafe in his body, in his culture, in his gender, in his career, and in his life.

Every time he fears disapproval, he leaks energy. Usually this person does not even notice the energy leaking from his body — but it leaks and leaves him depleted.

Another kind of leakage takes place in people who harbor sorrows from long ago. They leak energy from their heart. They do not realize that they have objectified love, placing it outside of themselves. When the love they sought did not manifest, they were heartbroken. If they never repaired the leakage in their hearts by recognizing that they were and are responsible for their feelings, then they still experience that leakage of energy from the heart.

The sheer volume of words that flow from the mouths of most individuals is another extraordinary leakage. Silence is a rare commodity in this world. People are given to babbling. They will babble things they do not know, babble things they do not believe, babble things that have no power, and babble things that have great power to reflect into their lives and create difficulties. This babbling is also leakage.

You leak energy when your mind gets on a treadmill and runs on and on about all of its theories, about all of the ways the intellect believes it can control your life. If you would have power, such leakage must be repaired.

Addictions to sex, cigarettes, alcohol, drugs, and food are all based on seeking something outside the self that will create a feeling of fullness and wholeness within. Because the search is outward-moving, leakage occurs. The leakage stops only when you realize that true fullness comes from within. Such fullness comes when one understands and inhabits Love.

Love is a deeply still beingness. It
is magnetic and coherent.

— *Solano*

Many believe that love is an outward-moving energy, but that is a misunderstanding. Love is still and regenerative. It grows from the deep recognition that one's being is essential in the universe. You are taught that love is an emotion that defines your relationship to others. You are taught further that love is sacrifice and possession. As a result, you probably believe that if you love everyone and everything, you will be rendered impossibly vulnerable and ineffective in the world. It is not so.

You experience a bridge-time as you move into the beingness of Love. In the bridge-time, you experience vulnerabilities. There are moments when you feel a fear of love. Sometimes you feel that to achieve what you want to achieve you have to express reproach, disapproval, anger, or judgment. You do not always know how to express yourself, remain in your center, and still be loving.

Some moments are graceless: you struggle to engage a new way of being, dwelling in the frequency of Love. Yet in the cusp time, most people still use such tools as intimidation, humiliation, and contraction.

However, the two ways of being simply cannot coexist. They cannot. When they begin to jockey for position in your life, there are times when you struggle to be loving, and yet you express yourself in ways that are not loving. But never fear: Ultimately, the ease and grace that come with inhabiting Love become more compelling, and the old ways fall away.

If you attempt to inhabit Love and you experience fear, the stakes are raised immeasurably in terms of what you have to gain. Your Soul, in such a moment, is calling you to your most advanced lessons. In that moment, you have the opportunity to move from one level of understanding to another. In such a moment, the most potent tool you have is stillness.

When my mother was in her late sixties, she developed Parkinson's disease. Her decline was accelerated dramatically when she fell and broke her hip, and the anesthesia administered during the hip replacement surgery, in combination with the Parkinson's drugs, resulted in psychotic behavior. It became apparent that she needed twenty-four-hour care, and that meant a nursing home.

I was living in California at the time, deeply engaged in pursuing my career as a filmmaker. I was working for a celebrity as the head of the production company. My life was full and exciting, and I felt that I was actually achieving what I had hoped and dreamed of all my life.

When I went to visit my mother in the nursing home for the first time, she begged me to take her home. She didn't want to be there. She wanted to be in the home that she had bought after my father's death.

The resulting emotion, for me, was fear of loving her. I was terrified that if I loved her in that moment, I would make decisions that would take away my ability to live the way I wanted to live, take away my freedom, take away my ability to fulfill myself. If I loved her, wouldn't I sacrifice my life, my dreams and desire, move back to my hometown and move in with my mother so she could live in her own home for the remainder of her days?

This kind of love, as I have come to understand it, is outward-moving love. It is a love that references the other person before referencing one's own Soul. Or, even more complex, the mind references the altered ego, fearing guilt or shame based on an expectation of one's self about loving someone else.

It was only when I dropped into the beingness of Love that all the chatter and recrimination stopped and I was able to look clearly at the situation. I took my mom back to her own home — something that I had been advised not to do by many people who had also heard her pleas. I helped her walk from room to room, through the whole house. She lay down on the couch, and after a bit she asked to be taken back to the nursing home. Though she never articulated it, I believe in that moment she, too, realized that living there was no longer possible.

Far more important than the situation itself was the experience of dropping out of the drama of love as an outward-moving energy, which could have motivated me to act in ways that would not have served either of us.

When one reaches the still point within,
Love as a state of being is achieved.

— *Solano*

Stillness does not require aloneness, nor does it require much time. It is rare to take time to be still when you are engaged with another, whether a shopkeeper or an intimate friend. It is rare that you stop and feel your Soul. Yet the moment you do, all the answers are made clear about how to inhabit Love and still move in the direction that your Soul urges. The answers manifest with an ease and grace that your altered ego would not have known and understood. Stillness is yours in the moment that you choose not to react. Stillness is available when you choose to drop into your Soul instead of following your known paths of communication.

Remember,
the Soul only knows Love.

— *Solano*

That is *all* the Soul knows: Love. The Soul's Love is what keeps you coherent as an individualized consciousness.

It is not what you outwardly do or say in a circumstance that shifts the energy. It is moving energy within your own body. No gesture, no word is necessary to signal that you have opened your heart. Energy shifts when you drop into your heart and become fully present in your body. When there is no resistance to the curriculum your Soul presents, you dwell in the place of authentic power. There, within, is the source of all apparent reality, and there all your reality is pliable. When you consciously, purposefully draw yourself to the place of authentic power, the dream that surrounds you will transform to match the Soul's values. In that moment, controversy, anger, and fear dissipate, and Love triumphs effortlessly.

A lovely young woman I know was living in New York City pursuing a career in acting. She was a regular meditator, and was using moments on the subway returning from an audition to drop into meditation. She felt someone sit down next to her, and when she glanced up she met the angry eyes of a youth who demanded that she give him all her money. Without hesitation she said to him, "I bless you from the God I Am." For a few tense moments, the young man stared at her, and then he abruptly got up and walked away.

When I asked her what had happened in that moment, she told me she didn't make a conscious decision, but rather felt that because she was in a still place, her Soul had spoken instead of her altered ego.

Remember, you possess all the tools
you need to repair your leakages.

— *Solano*

Whenever you experience a fear, or the addiction that accompanies fear, that emotion carries within it everything needed to render it no longer a source of leakage. You are not presented with an addiction or a fear or a leakage without a reason. Your Soul wants it presented to you. Your Soul wants it there. That is the Soul's way of bringing your conscious awareness to the place where power is available within you.

If you have confronted a neurosis day in and day out, year after year, your attention has been drawn to your greatest source of power. As you grow in wisdom, rather than slamming the door in the face of that neurosis, begin to open the door and invite the neurosis in. Your fear of the addiction, the habitual, will diminish as your identity becomes seated more fully in your Soul.

There is wisdom in such an approach. You become unafraid of yourself, unafraid of who you are. That fearlessness signals to the Soul that you are ready to hold all the power — that you truly are ready to wield it so that your life will be progressive.

Most people stumble when in crisis, when confronted with an illness or other circumstance they can't believe they have called to themselves. They resist its appearance in their life. That resistance signals to the Soul that the individual is not ready to fully embrace his inherent power.

Every time you reflect on events in your life and you think they are random, that they have nothing to do with you, *that* is the greatest leakage of energy you can have.

— *Solano*

The instant you acknowledge the precision, the perfection of what is happening, you stop being at the mercy of your created reality. You dwell at the place of cause, the place of authentic power. Embracing your challenges is the most potent means by which you can gain power and strength. A challenge appearing in front of you is an offering to you. It is an opportunity. It is a manifestation from your Soul, which is calling you out and saying, "Bring your whole self to what you have manifested. It will yield you up to your next moment and empower you more deeply. When you bring your whole self to that which you have manifested, you are empowered by a shield of light, a shield that is pure Love."

When individuals desire to know that they are Divine, all their addictions and fears begin to manifest more rapidly. One manifests on the heels of another.

One of the great addictions is to money. People desire money as a means of having control over their lives. You can work that formula, work it and work it, yet having money does not provide control over your life. Having money does not provide you with power. It is an illusion that power derives from money. Anyone who possesses a bit of money begins to understand the power of creation to some degree — but that power does not come from the money. The power manifests first.

The task is simple: When you find yourself captivated by fears about your bank account or your dotage or a desire to control the behaviors of others, when you yearn for money thinking it will provide the freedom you desire, you must drive yourself inward. This is when you realize that thoughts of money simply provide the map to the place of your greatest power and strength — the place of *cause* within you.

There was a man who couldn't resist spending money, and lots of it. If one set of sheets was good, then ten was better. Where one piece of art would be a perfect addition to his collection, he would buy five pieces. He just couldn't help himself. And he was viewed as a very powerful person. His books and seminars were very much in demand.

But the spending (leakage) caught up with him, and he lost nearly everything — except for what he couldn't lose: his ability to self-reflect. In his bankruptcy he recognized that he had been reduced to his essence — a raw, pure, and blazing energy. Now, because he had no way of leaking (his leakage was the addiction to acquiring more things), he was able to start holding the energy. It filled his whole being. He became even more clear and magnetic and awake and aware than he had ever been before. His needs for sufficiency — housing, travel, food, and clothing — were miraculously met, and he was happier and felt fuller than he had when he was fabulously wealthy.

The desires you feel are not who you are.

— *Solano*

Your desires provide you with a map. Maps tell you where you are so you can see where you need to go and arrive at where you want to be. The landscape of your life — your desires, your fears, and your addictions — show you where you are leaking energy. They show you ways that you can more authentically empower yourself to become a Soulful self generating a radiant light.

Your light field either grows or diminishes,
depending on whether you are leaking
energy or sustaining the energy within.

— *Solano*

Ask yourself if you feel energized or depleted by any given element in your life. If you apply this simple measure to every relationship, to every entertainment, to every fantasy, to every yearning, you will swiftly be able to identify what is a light-builder and what diminishes your light.

There are many opportunities to diminish your light. You live in such a way that all people are interdependent for approval and gain. As a result, you have many opportunities to experience emotions that diminish the light. Anger diminishes the light; fear, envy, jealously, lust, insecurity, and desire to control another all diminish the light. Only one thing increases the light: Love.

You desire love — the love of a mother, a father, a friend, an acquaintance, a life partner, or a sexual partner. Your desire places the source of love outside of yourself. When you become aware that you are projecting the love you want outside of you, then you can redesign the pattern. You've had moments when it felt as though love was being taken away from you. In such moments, your Soul's curriculum reveals itself, and the opportunity to experience God's Love is presented. In the moment you translate the experience of God's Love as your love of yourself, you become the Divine, loving you.

Within the experience of walking this path again and again, the heart ultimately recognizes that there is no love that is external. If you identify a source outside of yourself as the source of love, you leak energy. Then what you do is look to another and to another and to another. When you cease looking for love out there and begin looking inside your own being — when you love who you are and love your life — then you are inhabiting Love. When you inhabit Love, what do you think manifests before you?

Love manifests, and it replicates itself and propagates itself over and over again.

Remember, it is the love you embody that determines the quality of your life.

— *Solano*

When you recognize that the source of love, abundance, safety, health, and knowledge is within, your life changes. This healing must come forth to stop the leakage from the heart. Nothing comes from outside; it all comes from within. Shoring up places where there is leakage always requires the same process. You must identify anything that you place outside of yourself — to which you grant power — and reestablish the Source of that power within.

In order to repair an energy leakage, you must first acknowledge that your Soul has called you to your curriculum in this form — of the fear or addiction or unfulfilled longing that you are confronting.

Any moment that such emotion manifests, realize that it is your Soul's doing. It is calling you out (you are calling yourself out) and asking you to bring yourself creatively to a new understanding. It may seem harsh. Harsh lessons are legion here on Earth. There are those who stand in terror for their very lives. But fear is not a capricious expression of your Soul. Rather, in such an instance, your Soul is calling you out, asking if you are ready to stare at your temptation to fear, and to elevate it.

Pause at every temptation. Do not get busy, do not get on the phone, and do not try to blame it on someone else. Do not clean the house, do not pick up a book to distract yourself, do not turn on the television — stop in that moment and acknowledge. Recognize that you are being called out by your Soul.

The moment you feel anything other than love, the moment you feel a contraction, you are being called out by your Soul.

Recognize that *you are doing it to yourself*, not because you don't love yourself but because it is the most effective, most expedient way of repairing an energy leakage and empowering yourself. By calling you out, your Soul demonstrates the ways you hold yourself back, the ways you limit yourself. You mirror vulnerability to yourself so that you can gain strength in its place. Once you recognize this movement, you are able to bring yourself fully to the question of how you can meet your current fears creatively. You become seated in courage.

Next, acknowledge that your Soul calls you out to draw your attention to your greatest potential power. Rather than looking at your fears, addictions, or losses, and seeing them as vulnerabilities, acknowledge them as your greatest strengths. The Soul draws your attention to the leakage so that you might come into greater power.

Meeting fear as an opportunity to gain power causes the Soul to generate more light. When you meet fear as an opportunity to grow more aware of your Divinity, the Soul responds. You begin to master your fear in a way that feeds the body. The energy of the body is contained rather than leaking out.

Energy leakage causes you to lose power, to lose vitality in your physical life. The place in your body where you feel fear becomes the point of leakage. Physical weakness develops there. When the weakness becomes chronic, disease can develop there. Disease is another way that the Soul calls you out.

You must reclaim the power that you have invested in any other person or circumstance. Remind yourself that no one can give you the love or abundance or health or freedom or satisfaction that you seek. Repeatedly affirm that no one can take from you anything that can affect your wholeness.

When you walk through a situation in your imagination and you have no fear of loss or humiliation or violence, your heart can be open. When you have no specific expectations of the situation, you are able to be fully present and aware of the urgings of your Soul.

To seal the new containment of your energy, give thanks. In gratitude you are able to feel what it is to have energy contained rather than leaking out of your center. Contained energy gives you a sense of fullness; it comes not from an external source, but is generated from within.

You will find that each time you go through these steps, the leakage will diminish. More and more, you will experience yourself as an energy field held together by Love, the Love of the Soul. Then you grant yourself greater effectiveness and capacity to move you forward, accomplishing the things the Soul has laid before you as the curriculum for your life.

THE DREAM

What you experience as reality is
really just you dreaming.

— *Solano*

You believe that you were conceived and born, and that you were a baby who grew into an adult. You have the photographs and the bronzed baby shoes to prove it. Yet that is not what occurred. Furthermore, when it comes time for you to leave this reality and move to the next, you will not wither and die. These are games that your mind plays, because your mind is designed to build continuity, a story. It is designed to connect the dots, so to speak.

Between each of the events that occurs in your life — your journey from home to office, moving from one city to the next, or accomplishing a goal — your mind makes up a continual story thread, with a beginning, middle, and end. Your mind fits the story into the illusion of time.

This dream of life has laws, rules, and guidelines that have evolved. You have been part of the process of evolving the rules. Though you experience yourself as subject to the rules, *they* are really subject to *you*. In order for you to harness the power of your dream, you must grasp this idea: Though you experience your life here as a continuity that fits very neatly into the confines of time and space, this experience is utter illusion.

Time and space are not absolutes, and they are not the basis of the experience of change. This experience is based on thought processes and changing states of consciousness.

— *Solano*

Time and space are laws that humanity has created to explain the movement from one state of consciousness to another. When you begin to track movement from one state of consciousness to another, focusing on the movement more than the illusion of time, you hold the key to modifying your dream as you desire.

Your mind dreams that you walk or drive or fly from one place to the next. Your mind manufactures all the points along the way. It dreamed up your childhood and your adolescence, your marriage and your children.

The continuity in this process is that you, as a sentient, infinite Soul, are simply dreaming states of being. You are dreaming states of consciousness. At this moment, you are dreaming a state of consciousness in which you are contemplating the true nature of your being.

In this dream of being human, you are sorting out ways to explain to yourself how you got from babyhood to this point in your life. And you will do the same for the remainder of your time in this dream.

There are many implications of this principle. One of the greatest implications is that pain is not real. Fear is not real. Death is not real. Birth is not real. The intellect has a hard time grasping this insight. You see, the intellect tells you that it has proof that you fell and scraped your knee, and proof of the first time you made love. You have your scars and your trophies. But they are all dream stuff, too. The so-called proof is what the mind manufactures to explain the states of consciousness that you move through.

I have to admit that contemplating this information very rapidly causes fuses to blow in my intellectual mind. I have held loved ones as they died. I sat with my mother's body for hours after she died and it seemed pretty real to me, as did the pain she suffered up to the moment of her death. I have experienced pain and tragedy, and held newborn babies.

How can it be that pain and death and triumph are only illusions? The only way I can begin to wrap my mind around this concept is to stare at the apparent reality that surrounds me, and begin to see it through the lens of a pretend microscope — one that can reduce matter to its smallest parts: from molecules to atoms, to protons, neutrons, and electrons, and further to neutrinos and to the void that appears between particles. Did you know that most neutrinos passing through us come from the sun, and that trillions of neutrinos pass through the human body every second?

Contemplating such things, and contemplating things like radio waves and microwaves, television and cell phones, helps me begin to open my mind to the possibility that I am consciousness dwelling in a dream, and that I am held hostage in this dream by my agreement or belief in the rules of the dream. Yet I still wake up every morning and my feet hit the solid floor, and I am unable to walk through walls or fly like I can in the dreams I have while sleeping.

I am reminded of a Tolstoy quotation: "Our life is but one of the dreams of that more real life, and so it is endlessly, until the very last one, the very real the life of God." I value this invitation to expand the limits of my understanding of what I think of as reality, even though it requires a leap from my ordinary mental track to one that is quite a bit harder to sustain.

Your intellect is programmed to make sense out of this life, in which you are dreaming states of consciousness.

— *Solano*

The importance of knowing the intellect's role is not so that you cling to your history, or to urge you to focus on your individual perspective. From the perspective of individuality, you believe that people are born, live their lives, and die. This perspective generates an extraordinary amount of storytelling, along with the desire to get a grip on the process and control it.

As a result of your programming, you tell yourself stories about ambition at work, filling your bank accounts and emptying them, going on vacation. You struggle with your body, starving and gorging and striving to control it. Then, finally, you tell yourself the story that it is time to move out of this dream.

You live in a dream in which it is commonly held that the body is who you are. Most of your stories surround the body and how it is coping with the rules of this collective dream. But you have dreamed your body just as you have dreamed your history. You dream that people die and are no more. You dream that there are many forces that bear down on you here on Earth.

But there is only God: the Source of all that is. There are no separations in God; there are not even individual manifestations of God from God's perspective. Just as the cell on your right hand at the end of your index finger is part of your body, so are all parts of God part of that one force.

You have the free will to dream yourself as separate and unique. Yet even as you dream the dream of being separate, you seek to understand that you are God, wholly and completely. You strive to understand that everything you perceive in your dream is God.

Even now reading these words, you are dreaming. You are seeking to move from one state of consciousness to the next, in which you become aware of yourself as the dreamer.

When you embrace the awareness that you are the dreamer, you harness the power of the dream

— *Solano*

Embracing the awareness that you are the dreamer is another way you eradicate fear — then you begin to understand yourself as one with God. Understanding that you are one with God, you begin to see all events as purposeful. You begin to experience all elements of your dream as you, God, communicating with yourself.

Harnessing the power of your dream is a matter of relinquishing your history and your future.

— *Solano*

Harnessing the power of your dream requires relinquishing your dream judgments about the present moment. You think of your body as a mass that often seems to have a life of its own, but it is simply a collection of frequencies that is completely fluid.

The body obeys your mind's explanation of what you are doing in the various states of consciousness you inhabit. It is fluid. The greatest obstacle to this fluidity is your insistence upon drawing your identity from your history, grand or squalid or ordinary; or from the future you strive to attain, your goals and ambitions.

When you are seated in the now without judgment, you achieve the greatest fluidity of consciousness.

Your mind, making up the storyline of your life, designs the fabric of your body.

— *Solano*

You have dreamed up every detail of what you think of as reality to construct the story of your life. If you were able to hold this awareness in your thoughts and sustain it, you could command your dream to be precisely as you want it to be.

Recognizing that this reality is all a dream allows you to establish an observer, an internal eye that watches everything. Doing so, you begin to see how you build the storyline of your life, how you spin it. You also have the ability to recognize that when an individual dies, he does not actually go through pain. That is just an often-used storyline. It is true, the body may experience pain,. But you dreamt yourself into the experience of pain, and so you are capable of dreaming yourself out of it.

If you grasp that you are an infinite and indestructible essence, and you understand that your consciousness changes and builds the dream that you experience as your life, only one thing is left to understand: Why do you do it? What does it serve?

The answer is twofold. First, of course, it serves the curriculum that the Soul presents to move you into the knowledge of yourself as God. Second, the focus of cultural healing during the past several decades has been geared to teaching individuals how to love themselves. Moving from a state of consciousness in which you do not value yourself to one in which you love yourself is a very powerful step. Making this change allows you to recognize that even when you did not love yourself, you were still completely captivated and fascinated by who you are, by your dream.

If you were bored with this dream, you would not remain in it. But it compels you. It is a form of entertainment. It is a way for you to delight yourself. It is a way for you to grant yourself a means of moving into the awareness of yourself as the One, the Mystery, the Infinite, the Absolute — as God.

Sometimes you hit rough spots in your dream, where you experience arduous emotions. You may wonder what these emotions have to do with the process of coming to know that you are One with all that is.

What do you do when you are frightened? Fear is often what prompts you to try to understand your dream. It jolts you into active exploration of your state of consciousness. Fear is often what prompts an individual to the insight that everything is a dream. If it were not for fear, you would simply go along in your dream, delighted, entertained, and completely captivated by it. Fear is what prompts one to seek the Source.

Fear prompts in an individual the desire to move from one consciousness to another. Ultimately, the goal is to move into a consciousness where you can harness the power of the dream. In such a moment, the same creative power that provides you with fearful experiences can provide you with a mentor, a healer, a cathartic moment. The mind will build a connection between the two states of consciousness. The net effect is that you move from being ensnared in the dream to recognizing yourself as the dreamer, knowing that you are in charge of the dream.

Knowing that you are the dreamer and that you are in charge of your dream causes you to awaken within your dream.

— *Solano*

Early on in my process of trying to integrate what I was being taught, I began trying to have an out-of-body experience — the sensation of floating outside of one's body. I thought if I could do that, I would be able to shift my consciousness to identify with my Soul. I went through the exercise dutifully, time and time again. I would lie down and close my eyes, and envision being able to sit up out of my body and look down at my feet.

One afternoon, I went through the exercise and inexplicably found myself in the kitchen staring at the sink. I couldn't remember what I was doing there, so I walked out into the hall and down toward the living room. As I turned the corner, I saw my body lying on the couch, asleep. I was so overcome with a deep, passionate love for my body that I instantaneously returned to my body and jerked awake.

I had awakened in my dream of being human and had had a palpable experience of myself as the consciousness that is the Soul, outside the experience of myself as a human body.

Consider the death of the body. When an individual dies, relinquishing this dream body, she awakens in a new dream. In the new dream, she will express herself in a form that reflects the highest frequency of consciousness she was able to attain in her former dream realm. The individual will usually build a history for herself to explain how she found herself there. She'll build another history of having been a child with parents in some bucolic or terrifying circumstances. And in that dream, she'll have other conventions to work within, conventions that have been manufactured and agreed to.

It is the same here. You have awakened here from a previous dream. You are beginning to periodically touch the consciousness that this is a dream. Sometimes, you spike into an awareness in which you see the fabric of the dream. It is the quality of those spikes, the frequency attained that designs the dream realm you awaken in, beyond this dream realm.

You are forever. And dreaming forever and ever. The Bible says, "In my father's house are many mansions." So it is here on this level of dream reality, and in the infinity of dream realities that exist beyond this one. You have an infinite number of mansions and creations to wander in and to discover and to be utterly entertained by on your journey. Your dream may be one of glorious achievement. Whatever you dream, the dream is but one of the mansions provided for you by the Source.

You may choose to inhabit a new
dream at any moment.

— *Solano*

In building your dream and inhabiting it, you also dream the people who inhabit your dream and you provide a storyline for continuity. For most people, continuity does not come just from their history in this lifetime but includes past generations. These are all dreams. Shakespeare understood something when he wrote, "O God, I could be bounded in a nut shell and count myself a king of infinite space, were it not that I have bad dreams." — *Hamlet*, II.ii

Your genetics have been dreamed. The laws of the scientific community have been dreamed. That's not to say they aren't verifiable. In this dream, you can verify them, but they constantly evolve and change to suit the dream of evolving consciousness. Could the dream of cell phones and space travel have been held by group consciousness in the seventeenth century? Likewise, can the dream of teleportation or spontaneous regeneration of a limb exist in the twenty-first century? These things will come to be, as the laws of the scientific community evolve to suit the evolving group consciousness.

Science is not discovering the true nature of reality; you, the dreamers and your scientists as dreamers are dreaming the true nature of reality.

— *Solano*

Have you noticed that science fiction, born in the imagination, becomes science fact after a time? Science fiction inspires the group mind to dream new ways of being that eventually manifest as reality in this dreamscape.

The more you seek to pierce the fabric of the dream with your thoughts and to identify yourself as Divine, the more able you are to elect the state of consciousness that you desire for your entertainment. In this way, you are able to identify yourself as a Soul, forever dwelling in a dream realm in a dream body, but not trapped there.

Do you desire to harness the power of your dream? Do you desire peace? Do you desire to fully engage your creativity? Do you desire to know yourself as the Source of abundance in the universe? Do you desire to know yourself as the Source of all that is?

Then you are ready to invoke a state of consciousness in which you awaken within the dream and fully experience its fluidity.

You have arrived at the state of consciousness in which you are able to conceive this most powerful of understandings by dreaming, by conjuring up various mentors, teachers, and disciplines. But understand: You have generated each state of consciousness that corresponds to the appearance of these things in your life.

It is not the meditation or the chanting or the teacher or the healer that has generated the state of consciousness you now inhabit. It is *you*. Your Soul, moving you through your curriculum, is responsible for the consciousness you have attained.

You have generated a state of consciousness in which you awaken within the dream. You identify your life as a dream. You are coming to identify yourself as infinite mind, and you are beginning to see your body not as something solid, but rather as pure intelligence that articulates itself in dream form.

As you now strive to awaken more fully in your dream, you can expedite matters by remembering that you are the dreamer. You are God. You are the Infinite Mystery. You are the One that articulates itself as the many, and as this dream.

When you are still, seek the Source of your dream. Seek to know where it is being projected from. Breathe into each moment, realizing experientially that the moment is all there is. In this way, you, the dreamer, can become one with the Source of all your dreams.

It is in stillness that you are able to feel yourself as the center of the universe.

— *Solano*

The linear mind often finds it confusing to contemplate being the center of the universe. It questions: "If I am the center of the universe, then what does that make everyone else?" The answer is that they, too, are the center of the universe — you all inhabit the same space. You all inhabit the same Absolute.

"*In an infinite universe, every point can be regarded as the center, because every point has an infinite number of stars on each side of it*"- Charles William Johnson, from *Hawking's A Brief History of Time, A Commentary.*

When you contemplate yourself as the center of the universe, you gather all of your dreams into that moment and dwell in the dream of your life, nonlinearly. Thought drops from intellect into Soul-based experience. Your linear mind allows you to spin the dream out into a story. And your linear mind, with its unique talents, allows you to fill in the blanks between states of consciousness.

Perhaps this all seems easy to comprehend just now. Perhaps you are generating a field of consciousness in which you can grasp that this is a dream, that it is all fluid, that there is no past or future. There is only God, and you are it. Yet tomorrow you may awaken and live in your dream as you are dreaming it, filling in the blanks between states of consciousness, connecting the experiences of bank accounts being empty and full, connecting between fulfillment and lack, between loss and gain.

The task then becomes to awaken more frequently in the dream, which is the precursor to being completely and fully awake. The key to awakening more often is in understanding the purpose of the dream. As you recall, the dream is for your entertainment. You dwell in this specific dream because the material for entertainment is rich. Separating yourself out into a multiplicity is a unique and exquisite way of entertaining yourself.

When you find yourself generating a state of consciousness that you do not desire — that is the moment to stop. That is the moment to wake up! Remind yourself that you are dreaming and that the dream is fluid. The moment you do so, your perspective will shift. If you are clear enough and drive your awareness deep into the place that generates the dream material, the dream will change.

All things exist in the same moment
and occupy the same space.

— *Solano*

Most individuals are aware that they exist, but they do not necessarily recognize that they function as a part of a greater body of intelligence. People are continually responding to the greater body of intelligence, but they do not know on a conscious level. Being engaged with the group mind is like that.

Most likely you did not get up this morning and think to yourself: I will dress a certain way because that is how I am supposed to dress in this culture given the constraints of gender, class, ambition, and so forth. You probably only considered what clothes you own that you particularly like and that fit the circumstances. But beneath these considerations are all the constraints derived from the group mind.

Many other things are derived from the group mind. Many of your attitudes and opinions about yourself, your life, and others in your life are a result of the group mind. Many of your attitudes and opinions about what constitutes success and a life well lived derive from the group mind. The group mind factors into the dream you are dreaming because a group dream is taking place. The group dream has created the dream of planet Earth. It has orchestrated the environment here. It has designed the evolution of the species to become a complex creation, and it is continuing to evolve. A body in this century is very different from a body a century ago or ten centuries ago or a thousand centuries ago. Why? Because thought, when expressed into the medium in which you are creating, alters the fabric of the dream.

Here it is important to make a distinction between the conscious and subconscious states of mind. The life that the Soul leads is in the subconscious, and it is accessible at any given moment. Communication from this part of yourself sometimes comes through your dreams and intuitions. The Soul has a broader perspective; it views itself as a part of a greater body, part of the medium that is God.

The Soul's view can compassionately and fearlessly send you into a situation in which you will experience rugged emotions. Such experiences allow you to grow into full awareness that you are Divine. If you were to examine, fearlessly, what was gained through such emotions, you would value those emotions more. If, prior to engaging in situations of intense emotion, you could bring to conscious awareness the reason your Soul needs them — and meet that need — then you would have no need to walk into the situation.

All emotions provide you with a reflection of the frequency, the tone, that you are dwelling in.

— *Solano*

Everyone has his primary tone, his vibratory frequency. That tone is a mixture of conscious thought and thoughts that dwell at the Soul level, the subconscious level.

Many people have Soul urgings that the altered ego will not recognize. This lack of acknowledgment is a willful act on the part of the altered ego, which tends to rigidity, whereas the Soul is utterly and completely pliable. The Soul is complete in its embrace of all that is, because it knows itself to be indestructible. It knows itself to be engaged in an entertainment.

When you recognize that every experience — even the experiences that you take the most seriously — is for your entertainment, you gain the ability to participate with a sense of play.

You must leap fully into the embrace of complete understanding that God is who you are.

— *Solano*

Even when people have been on a path of self-discovery for years, their language still might betray a deep-seated belief that God is outside of them. Intellectually, they know that God dwells within but this concept has not made its way down to the level of visceral knowledge. Grasping this concept, however, is absolutely fundamental to making the evolutionary leap.

Examine your language about the true nature of your being. Examine how you think about yourself in relation to the Divine. This self-reflection is crucial to embracing the Soul's curriculum. Seating your identity in the Soul, inhabiting the Soul's infinite, timeless perspective provides the ability to keep the altered ego under surveillance and provides the guidance necessary for the altered ego to agree and consciously participate in the evolutionary leap. You must drive the knowledge that *you are one with the Divine Intelligence* deep into your viscera. The more you practice this response, the more the altered ego ceases to shrink from the experiences that the Soul designs.

When you fully embrace the understanding that you are God, and therefore are One with all that is, you embrace your capacity to change the course, direction, texture, and experience of the group dream.

— *Solano*

Think about the times in your life when you felt this heightened understanding, however briefly. These times are a peak, a spike in the frequency of thought in which you normally live. That elevated thought, even if momentary, shifts the mean — the average — of thought in the group dream.

The shift that takes place in your culture as a result of your elevated moment reverberates into the medium that is the larger context: the universe. Your desire to understand that you are dreaming impacts your life by drawing into your dream experiences that move you along in your process. As it gathers momentum, the process connects you to others who are also elevating their thought processes.

You are growing in understanding your power to change your culture, and your culture reflects that growth. Television and the Internet are good examples. Your ability to know what is taking place around the globe at any given moment and to interact with others is unprecedented. People are reacting differently to this revolutionary change. Some are embracing it as positive growth that ultimately educates the societal mind and causes it to advance. But those who are identified with altered ego tend to rigidity. They are trying to hold back the tide. The trend toward practicing fundamentalist religion is, in many cultures, a reflection of this tendency to rigidity, which is the desire to hold back the tide of cultural evolution.

An example of cultural evolution is embodied in the potential of genetic engineering and human cloning, which are extremely taboo in this culture. Many believe that humanity is not responsible enough to have such power. However, education, knowledge, and advancement through such experimentation cannot be held back. It cannot. Rather, greater responsibility must accompany the power that is gained.

The sense of that responsibility is growing. It grows in your societal Soul, and the societal Soul sees to it that circumstances conspire to instill the responsibility. You probably know people who drank and smoked and took drugs and stayed out all night when they were in college. And now? Now most of them eat right, drink very little, and are in bed by ten and up with the dawn. It's a matter of understanding the dream that you are dreaming, dwelling in the body, and being responsible for the frequency you generate with your thoughts.

If a person is not responsible to the frequency she is generating with her thoughts, what do you suppose happens? More education.

Another example of this process, and one that hits a very raw nerve, is the horror of the Jewish Holocaust. Hitler and the Third Reich revealed a profound vulnerability in the group mind and in societal evolution. His reign of terror coincided with the advent of television and the atom bomb, two of the most significant scientific breakthroughs in the twentieth century. His life has become a cautionary tale that reverberates in societal consciousness to this day. *Never again* is the message of that tale. That message is a gift.

If you step back from the horror, from those whose lives were sacrificed, if you step back and look at each of those Souls (including Hitler himself) and remind yourself that they are fulfilling their Soul's curriculum, that their Souls live on, you encounter another reminder that they all dreamed a dream. They dreamed it on behalf of the group mind.

The dramatic lessons of the Holocaust reverberate in this dream, and they will reverberate for many, many dreams to come. These valuable lessons offer us education and cultural evolution.

I have to admit that I had a real problem with this last lesson. I have seen too many apparently inexplicable tragedies and traumas suffered by the dearest, kindest, most loving and wonderful people to glibly proclaim, "Well, it was their Soul's curriculum." So, as I was presented with this lesson, I took it into my meditation. I looked first at a dear friend who died at age twenty-nine of breast cancer. She was an elementary school teacher, beloved by her students, family, and friends alike. When she was ill, I heard all kinds of explanations about it. One psychic told her that she had died in the Holocaust and had been reincarnated, and that the site where the disease had manifested was where she had suffered mortal wounds while in Auschwitz. Huh? So she came back and was suffering again?

So in my meditation, I looked at the very end of her life. A man fell in love with her. He knew she was ill, but they moved in together and he loved, adored, and cared for her to the very end. Even though she was ill, she was very happy. I looked at that, and I looked at the people whose lives she touched, the healing her family went through, and the impact she had on others even in her illness, and I began to see patterns emerging, patterns of progress and of wisdom gained.

Another friend, a dancer, brilliant and generous, gentle and kind, died in a tragic accident when hit by a train. What was the value in that? What did his Soul have in mind for that? Isn't it possible that the universe is just a random, chaotic place where innumerable acts of violence and love take place, and where all are met with the same indifference?

Again, I took my friend's life and death into my meditation and asked to be shown how his Soul could have gained from such an experience. And again, I was shown a broader perspective on his life, on the energy that he released in his life, and on the energy that was released in the aftermath of his death. There were relationships that began, relationships that were clarified, people who were inspired, and movement that was prompted as a result of his death. Those elements were observable. But I was also shown things in my meditations that I could not verify, things that had to do with my friend's relationship with Souls who were not in bodies, with whom he had agreements and appointments after his human life ended.

I went on with this process. I still find experiences in peoples' lives that seem to defy explanation or justice, until I back far enough away from the pain and horror to begin to see the lines of energy that extend from the experience. Then I can begin to see some organization, some rhythm or pattern — and from there see value gained in the form of wisdom or progressive movement.

There are dreams within dreams.

— *Solano*

Gaining emotional balance in the dream — your life — that exists in the context of the overarching dream of humanity, is achieved by becoming fully identified with your Soul's wisdom.

Your DNA — the dream material that is affected by the progression of your thoughts and by the group mind — was conceived, built, and evolved in relationship to the group mind. Your genetics have provided you with this body, which had a particular resonance at birth.

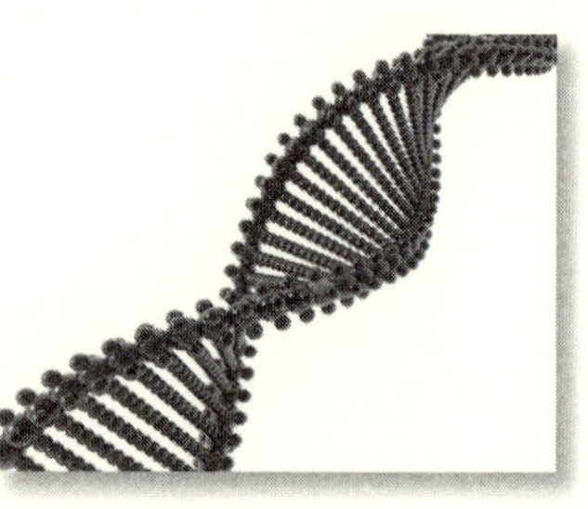

That resonance was a combination of your genetics and your particular Soul's imprint upon the body that you built. As your body grew in the matrix of your family, your community, your nation, and your world, certain emotional patterns were reinforced.

As you have engaged in life's challenges, you have desired growth from yourself. You have grown physically, sometimes relationally, sometimes emotionally, but you have been moving and growing. That movement reveals which emotional patterns are body-based and which are altered ego-based.

When you identify emotions that are body — and altered ego-based — you hit upon the things that are most challenging to transform. You then begin pushing against boundaries that have been put in place by your participation in the group mind, the group dream. These boundaries are characterized by fear, anger, doubt, insecurity, and the sense that you have to compete for every good thing you manage to create in your life.

Competition and aggression define such boundaries. They are characterized by the belief that you are a human being encased in a body, taking care of self *first and foremost*, and your tribe or community secondarily. These emotional patterns are counterproductive to transformation. When, in order to achieve transformation, you resist the inclination to move into the values of aggression and competition, you are more than halfway to the balance you seek. The other half of the battle comes from learning how to drop down into the Soul's values in order to produce the reality you desire.

When you become fully who you are, when you fully inhabit your Soul, opportunities for joyous, creative interaction are compelled to you effortlessly by your Soul.

— *Solano*

Consider again the experiment with the magnet under a piece of paper, and the metal filings sprinkled over it. The filings arrange themselves into a pattern that reveals the invisible electromagnetic field of the magnet. This experiment offers an excellent illustration of what it is like for us to be Souls dwelling in a pliable medium.

Mastery of your dream happens when you become fully who you are. Rather than trying to move away from the magnet and make the metal filings adapt to a specifically chosen pattern, it is far more effective to *be* the magnet. What happens on the two-dimensional surface above the magnet also happens in all dimensions around the magnet.

Striving to make someone behave as you want him to behave is like the magnet trying to move out of itself in order to arrange the metal filings. The place for you to dwell is where you drop into the Soul self that organizes and orchestrates all experiences around you. Drop into that place and let the Soul continue to deliver. Let it continue to bring everything to you.

When you find yourself doubting that you have the linear knowledge or the endurance or the personality to engage the dream that is already manifested around you, drop out of it. Drop out of that battle. Do not even engage it. Do not try to convince your altered ego. Do not try to convince your personality. Drop out of it, and drop into the source of magnetism. In this way, you can compel intuition and knowledge.

When you walk into circumstances with new people, there is a level at which you know what is going on in that room, and a level at which you do not. You want to dwell in the level at which you know what is going on; that is the level of the Soul. At the Soul level you are not buffeted about by all the various agendas of the people in the room; you are not engaged with their altered egos and their personalities, all attempting to compel or to manipulate their dreams.

It is crucial for you to understand this point. It is urgent, not only for your own individual life and what it is you are trying to achieve, but also for what is possible here on Earth.

When you dwell identified as Soul first, you become
a part of the force that drives societal evolution.

— *Solano*

By living as Soul first, you begin to affect cultural change. You begin to have an effect on the group mind by inhabiting your Soulfulness: the state of consciously being guided by your Soul's values. Your Soul desires to provide this guidance on your behalf, and on behalf of the group dream as well.

Soulfulness grows out of living as one who is a knower, one who possesses and values intuition. Living this way, you do not walk away from an awkward conversation thinking it a useless waste of time. That reaction is the altered ego talking. You drop down into the Soulfulness of your being, knowing that in every moment you impact the evolution of God's expression. This knowing is not something that the altered ego can grasp, but the Soul does.

Dwelling in your Soulful, intuitive self, you raise the bar for yourself in your interaction with others. You give yourself useful tools to achieve balance in every interaction, intimate or social.

The state of consciousness you inhabit, your light field — who you are — not what you say or do, has the greatest impact on the group dream. In a room full of people where you do not utter a word but are present and Soul-identified, your light field affects the mean frequency in that room. In a conversation or a family interaction, if you are identified with your Soul and its values, you are able to see the basis of the interaction more clearly, and therefore you interact with an open heart. That openness shifts the frequency of the interaction. Just as the oceans were created drop by drop, so each interaction contributes to the larger body of human consciousness.

A conscious individual is inspired to action (or inaction) by his or her Soul.

— *Solano*

Some interpret the notion of dwelling in Soulfulness as an injunction to passivity. The simplest way of understanding Soulfulness is to remember that it operates like a force of nature: There is a time to blow like a hurricane and there is a time to be gentle.

When faced with a challenging situation where you don't know how to react, dwell in your Soul. If what you feel to do is wait before acting, then the action of waiting alone is appropriate. If, in the same instance, you drop down into your Soul and are moved to speak or act, then acting upon that impulse is correct.

Only when a response is habitual, activated by fear, or impelled by the altered ego alone — as a result of desire for a particular learned response — will you act without wisdom, and stumble. The difference between being in your Soul and being in your altered ego is determined by the quality of the information that you receive. Motivation from the Soul has a deep resonance, whereas the altered ego's drives have a more brittle, more rigid resonance. The altered ego's resonance is associated with a contracted heart.

When you act in response to the altered ego, you will stumble, and experience discomfort and chaos as a result. Such errors are the way the Soul teaches us, because the Soul realizes that if you are going to be wise, you must be able to recognize the difference between these impulses.

Whatever it takes, the Soul will manifest the lessons necessary for you to learn that dwelling in the Soul is the only sustainable way of being.

— *Solano*

Your Soul is your teacher. Everything that happens to you — everything, every circumstance that arises — is the Soul at work in your life, orchestrating the dream so that you lift your vibratory frequency. When your electromagnetic field begins to vibrate at a higher frequency, your desired experience of yourself and your dream begin to match.

Everyone would like the experience of dwelling on this planet in utter delight. Whatever blocks your Soul from being able to arrange that experience for you will be revealed over and over again. Maintain, at the forefront of your consciousness, the understanding that this reality is all a dream, that the dream is pliable, and that everything you experience is ordained by the Soul for your growth.

If you review your memories, which are simply states of consciousness, and identify every major event in your life — every loss, joy, betrayal, victory, death, illness — as your Soul's manifested reality (as opposed to your linear memory) you will experience a shift in perspective. That shift will create a new history for you. Your view of your life will shift. You will not be able simply to sleepwalk through the day feeling victimized or afraid. Such attitudes will no longer be able to exist; they will give way to the understanding that *your Soul is dreaming your life with a curriculum*. The curriculum is designed to move you to a state of consciousness in which the way you want to feel and the dreamscape that has organized itself around your magnetic field match.

You have dreamed the Souls that populate your life. They are dreaming you; you are dreaming them. You are compelled by your life. It is just as compelling to you whether your life is one of delight, abundance, and ease, or one of horror, abuse, and fear.

Every event in your life, in fact, your entire existence, has occurred for your entertainment.

— *Solano*

When something loses its entertainment value for you, it can no longer remain in your dream. Period. No exceptions.

In order to stay awake in the dream, you need only remind yourself of the principle that everything is happening for your entertainment. The realization of this principle prompts you to remember your curriculum, which in turn sparks the remembrance that everything that manifests is symbolic.

Your manifestations symbolize the tone and quality of your magnetic field. Your magnetic field is symbolic of your consciousness. Your consciousness is the blend of your Soul, altered ego, personality, and genetics, all interacting with one another. The altered ego, the personality, and your genetics are temporal; they, too, are just symbols in your dream. But the Soul always triumphs. Always. Because it is forever.

Desire and fulfillment are different sides of the same coin.

— *Solano*

Many people are confused about how to sort out what is the Soul's desire, and what is the altered ego's desire. That confusion reveals itself most dramatically when you seek to determine what is appropriate to desire of another person. Your will cannot trespass on others without their having a dream of their own that has called in that experience. Now let's elevate the question.

If you are called by your altered ego into an interaction with another that he experiences as a trespass, and his emotions reverberate back to you as though you have trespassed, then your Soul has manifested the experience in order for you to grow. The Soul desires that you understand what drove you to the interaction that generated a sense of trespass in another.

The questions you must ask are these: What attitudes drove you to that experience? What value is there in feeling shame, guilt, or unworthiness? What perspective must change in order for you to heal the sense of lack? What do you need to know in order to release the patterns of using your will, your altered ego, and your personality to make something happen?

The Soul is asking you to examine how your altered ego views the dream in which you manifest your life. If your altered ego's perspective is that there is not enough, that you must make someone else agree to fulfill something for you, your life is likely to be a struggle. That perspective is not the Soul's.

I am reminded of a woman who came to me periodically to work on jealousy. Her husband was a man who was attractive and talented and who was a very free spirit. He loved to play with his sexuality in a very provocative way and thought nothing of walking up to the edge of a sexual liaison but would always keep his agreement to monogamy.

This behavior was very foreign to the woman, very threatening to her. Yet, her husband didn't feel that there was any "trespass" on the integrity of their relationship and couldn't understand why the woman felt disrespected and diminished by such actions. The husband felt that she was being unreasonable when she became upset by his actions. He felt that her reaction trespassed on his ability to express himself freely.

Both of them loved one another deeply but found that they could not find a way to settle this difference. Ultimately, what they each came to realize is that both expressions — the jealousy and the husband's need to seduce others — were born of lack. Their Souls brilliantly manifested this repeated upset in order to draw their attention to a place of authentic, centered, grounded power.

When this awareness entered the dialogue, mutual care and respect began to grow in place of the existing dynamic, allowing them to hold on to their connection to their center even when challenging situations arose. This recognition provided them a means of navigating away from the need for another person — her for her husband and his for others — to fulfill their sense of lack.

Imagine, if you will, that the dream in which you live is a box canyon. You go to the edge of the box canyon and you shout into it: "I DESIRE!" What do you think you are going to hear echoed back? You are going to hear "I DESIRE!" If you go around all the time saying to yourself, "I need, I want, I wish I had," the tone of those mantra-like thoughts will reverberate back into your life like an echo. And if you go around behaving as though you lack, lack will reverberate back into your life.

Such affirmations are the antithesis of connecting with your Soul and shouting into the canyon, "FULFILLMENT IS MINE." The Soul knows fulfillment and is capable of bringing it to you.

Let's broaden this idea a bit. When you find yourself needing to have the agreement of another individual or group in order to fulfill a desire, you can go about securing that agreement in many different ways. The *least* effective way is by engaging the altered ego, and struggling and striving to secure agreement from other altered egos and personalities. The *most* effective way is by dropping down into your Soul, and recognizing and embracing fully where you are in your curriculum. Then generate the state of consciousness that enables you to feel fulfilled by your desires rather than to feel diminished by them.

Let's say that you are not in a relationship, but want to be. The altered ego says that something you want is not there. As a result of this lack, in combination with the way you have been indoctrinated in your culture, you desire a relationship, you crave it, you want it, you need it. You continually ask yourself, "Where is it?" You are shouting into the box canyon, "I DESIRE," and you are going to hear back, "I DESIRE." You are going to keep getting desire, desire, and more desire.

What you must do instead of reacting to your perceived lack is drop down into your Soul to seek the relationship, the project, the career, the fulfillment that you desire. When you drop into your Soul, you recognize the ways you are fulfilled experientially already. Consider the times you have experienced states of consciousness in which you fulfilled a particular desire. If there are none, then engage your imagination. First, of course, you recognize that God the universe, God, who you are, IS everything you desire. You only desire a relationship because you desire to know yourself as God. You only desire to get that job because you desire to know yourself as God. You only desire the money, the beauty, the freedom because you desire to know yourself as God. And you are already that. You are already God.

Recognize that every fulfillment is
within you this moment.

— *Solano*

You push on the flexible, pliable stuff of this dream, you desire things to come and arrange themselves around you, because such actions will reveal you to yourself.

Take the short cut. Generate the feeling of fullness, of richness, of love of yourself. Embrace yourself, give yourself the recognition. Then go with that feeling, even if it is only a shred at first, and shout into the box canyon, “I have a shred of fulfillment!” You will get back, “I have a shred of fulfillment!” and that is a start. You can build upon that shred, and then go shout about that.

Now is all that exists.
In the now, all there is is fulfillment.

— *Solano*

You are utterly and completely fulfilled in this moment. It is already done. It will always be that way, for all there is is God, and you are that. The entertainment takes place in this dream, and beyond this dream are infinite other realities. But all of it takes place in the now. When you drop into your being and experience yourself seated in the present, you are wholly embracing yourself as a Soul.

The relationship between the present and what manifests in the next moment is simply this: The frequency you generate in the present reconfigures the field around you — the unique and specific manifestation of God that you are. This reconfiguration allows another dream to appear before you. The more you understand future and past as constructs of the altered ego and personality, the more you are able to fully inhabit the present moment. And the more you will be able to feel your access to fulfillment. Fulfillment is always there.

It is by being in the present moment that you receive the lavish and complete support of the Soul.

— *Solano*

Being seated in the present moment, you experience the support provided by the Soul. This support drives you toward a complete experience of knowing yourself to be God and knowing yourself to be fulfilled.

And what of death, by far the greatest gravity in this dream? Most people fear it. When they contemplate death, they are thrown into a panic about what their experience of it will be like. The fear of death is what most commonly pulls people out of the now. They wonder whether it will be painful, whether they will still be a coherent consciousness after death; they wonder what they will do on the other side. They wonder if they will find themselves horribly alone and frightened, or if they will find themselves in the bosom of God.

I would remind you again: None of this is real. Birth is not real. You move from one state of consciousness to another, and you build the continuity that connects states of consciousness.

With the knowledge that life and death are illusions, you achieve the ability to bring yourself back to the now when fear presses in. When you bring yourself back to the present, you are able to access the deep, abiding foreverness that is your Soul. When you are in a state of conjecture about what will be, or remorse about what has been, you are not seated in the center of your creativity. Return your thoughts to your center, to your now, and the balance required to move into a new state of consciousness is yours.

The signature of your light field is your prayer.

— *Solano*

Your life — the way you live it, the way you view reality — is like a walking prayer. You are constantly in prayer. What you create in your dream is a direct result of your prayer. It is urgent that you understand what you are praying for. If you are able to move with your prayer, to lift it, to articulate your desires more precisely, your dream will change instantly.

The echo illustration serves here, too. If you go to the brink of a cliff overlooking a box canyon and shout out your prayer, and it is, "I desire fulfillment," you are going to hear back, "I desire fulfillment." If you go to the brink and say, "I am afraid of not having money," you will receive that expression back. Your fear and your desire reverberate back to you. You can desire and desire and desire, and all you will get back is desire. So you must refine your prayer.

Here is how it works: Consider the proverbial pebble in the pond. You are the pebble, and the

waves are the results of your tone — your constant prayers coming back to you. What happens is even more instantaneous than this example indicates, however. The very instant you inhabit a state of consciousness — whether it is the knowledge that you are rich or that you are fearful — the dream in which you live immediately answers your prayer in kind.

The dream you live in is a pliable medium. You can push upon it and it will yield; it is flexible. Your life is not fixed; it is pliable. Even though you have gone through change after change after change, you are not there yet, so your task is to be willing to change again. The necessary change is to inhabit a state of consciousness in which you can walk to the brink of the cliff and shout out "Abundance," and have "Abundance" reverberate back. You shout out "Love," and "Love" is what reverberates back; "Fulfillment," and "Fulfillment" reverberates back. That is how it is in this dream.

Your task, in your meditations, in your conversations, in your deep contemplations is to understand what your living, breathing prayer is. If you are not satisfied with your prayer, you can transform it.

Effective prayer is the act of becoming one with the state of consciousness that you desire to inhabit, and being steadfast in it.

— *Solano*

I met with a woman who had a number of degrees after her name. She was an accomplished violinist who had performed around the world and had recorded several albums, yet she was dissatisfied with her life. Through a series of choices, she was supporting herself largely through teaching, and she was living in a city not particularly known for its music scene.

As a result of our working together, examining her walking prayer, she was able to identify the state of consciousness she wanted to inhabit — one of vibrant creativity rewarded by abundance and opportunity. She stopped playing violin and turned all of her attention and focus to art and design. Within a short time, she began to produce one amazing painting after another. She parlayed that achievement into a successful career as an interior designer, with projects in such places as California, New York, Martha's Vineyard, London, and Dubai. It was mind-boggling how quickly her dream changed once it was examined, once her walking prayer was understood.

But that wasn't the end of her transformations. After a few years, she found herself living in London and longing to play violin again. She turned her attention back to the instrument with renewed inspiration. The music community there embraced her, and within a matter of months she was on the slate at The Royal Albert Hall.

Her life exemplifies how fluid the dream material is, how by understanding your walking prayer, you can transform it.

All too often people inhabit a state of consciousness that they have dwelled in for so long they forget they can inhabit another one. Fear is the predominant tone of this culture. That said, all things are working together synergistically so the creativity of God is constantly being served.

There is such fervor now, a polarization of the group consciousness; it is galvanizing the culture and will sweep in many changes. These changes will shift the way the Earth and its resources are viewed — even the resource of other human beings on the planet. The changes will affect your life, as you are called upon to actively change your dream.

Your relationships with others and the use of your power — the power of the intellect, the power of your knowledge, the power of your ability to drop into the dream and change the past and the future — will bring about sustainable systems, sustainable commerce, and sustainable governments in the generations to come. These changes will come from corporations. Corporations will be the source of changes from which sustainability will grow, changing the face of the planet and the group dream.

You only need to look at the generations that are growing up. As a group, these generations hold the Earth as something precious that appears to be diminishing. And their numbers are growing, not arithmetically, but geometrically. They are moving into positions of power. Corporations cannot reach into the pool of employable talent without engaging this new generation. These Souls are moving into positions where they are capable of making the difference. In very short order, a trend will emerge in the corporate realm to eliminate waste, to eliminate depletion of resources, and to discover the means of building up resources rather than depleting them. Why? Because it will serve their bottom line.

Most people in the corporate culture have, in their dreams, needed to serve their superiors and their boards, whose only concern was how much profit they could generate. They were not concerned with where it was coming from. As a result, they galloped on. Now there is nowhere left to gallop to. And so, it has all funneled down to this moment. That is why it is valuable for you to understand the dream you are dreaming. Dream in such a way that the prevailing culture becomes one that understands that every Soul is God's Soul. In dreaming it such, you will render it such.

Your Soul is constantly communicating with you,
even when you are unaware of the communication

— *Solano*

The Soul has a language all its own. Learning the Soul's language is one of the best means of shaping your dream. If you view everything as a portrait that is bearing you a message, then you have an immediate inroad to the language of the Soul. There is no random occurrence, not a random word, not a wasted gesture, not a waste of sensation. The moment that seems most innocuous is rife with communication from your Soul. Your Soul is the *center* of your being — it is the intelligence that generates the entirety of what you perceive as your life.

Begin to think from your center, to act from your center, to engage others from your center. You'll find many different levels of communication going on: not just the words, the words are the least of it. The words are simply to engage your linear mind.

Notice your response the next time you come into contact with someone new. You may feel something different — perhaps it is unease, perhaps it is attraction. Rather than thinking about the encounter, making up stories about it, let yourself perceive the meeting with your center — understanding that your Soul is simply creating a portrait in order to move you into a state of consciousness. In this way, you will more easily understand the message your Soul is presenting in the form of the person in front of you.

As a result of this practice, you will become a more Soulful being. You will become more present-oriented. You'll become aware that you are receiving information all the time. Thinking with your center allows you to see the metaphors that are presented to you.

There are several ways that individuals sleep through their lives. One is when the intellect becomes so busy with all it is trying to understand that it fails to notice the patterns; another is when the mind becomes so involved in the intricate delight of its creativity that it fails to notice what is being generated and experienced by the center.

Ideally, the linear mind (left brain), the creative mind (right brain), and the center (Soul) operate in concert, increasing intelligence exponentially. In concert, they enable you to access your intuitive self, to merge with the source of all dreams.

There is only One Source. All potential flows from that One.

— *Solano*

This dream is governed by certain rules, which are accepted, agreed upon, and affirmed by the group mind every day. The rules are created by the group mind. When you became identified as individuals, you collected yourselves together and, like a school of fish that darts this way or that, or a flock of birds that dances as the sun is setting, you moved together. Whenever one separates from the flock, that action will affect the flock because of the nature of its energetic interplay in that flock. If you are to dream a new dream, then be like the one bird that separates

itself out from the flock — listening to something other than the beating of the wings of other birds.

Listen to and seek to understand foreverness, your nature as infinite intelligence. By so doing, you merge with the dream in which you live. Once you have merged with the dream, you discover that it is utterly and completely yielding. The dream is pliable to one who understands that the infinite intelligence supports and allows this dream. From that awareness, everything is yours to create as you wish: your history, your future, and certainly your now. Merging with the dream is the portal through which you access perceived past and future.

All things then become subject to your design. The group mind agrees that a room is filled with chairs and bodies. Really, the room is just space with particles that are filled with space, moving in a frequency that creates a wave. The wave has a signature that creates the illusion of a solid, a liquid, or a gas.

Even so, there is only one fundamental thought intelligence: God. Out of God grows all this creativity and all this diversity. You are dreaming this moment. You have articulated the faces of those around you, in much the same way that you enter dreamtime in sleep. There, entire worlds are created, replete with their own design, their own textures, their own themes, their own colors, their own dynamics, their own fragrances, and their own rules.

Yet you make a distinction between sleeping dreams and the waking dream, saying that while you are awake you are engaged in reality but when you are asleep you are dreaming. You say you know the difference because here, if you cut yourself, you will bleed. Here, you supposedly can't fly; people supposedly don't change form before your very eyes. But all of those things — and more fantastic things — happen in your nighttime dreams. Most people have had the experience of commanding slumber dreams to change, and having them do so. It is within your capability to change your waking dreams, just as you change your nighttime dreams.

The fluidity of your nighttime dreams is a wonderful training ground. Training yourself to remember your nighttime dreams is an excellent place to begin understanding the dream that is your life. By training yourself to remember your dreams, you train yourself to change them with your will. Frequently, in the course of a day, remind yourself that you are dreaming, that everything you see is dreamed, and that it is but God communicating.

The value of knowing that you are dreaming and being able to change your dream is this: As a result of coming to this knowledge, you contribute dynamically to the entirety of the consciousness that is God. You, as God, dreaming God, coming to greater awareness that you are God affects the evolution of all consciousness.

It is an auspicious moment in your evolution. This moment is when the capacity to align what you think, what you hope, and what you design presents itself. This alignment will bring you the precision of what your Soul intends your experience of life to be.

There is only God; that is all there is. God articulates itself into all the multiplicity that composes the universe. Your life, your beingness, is derived from God. Most people are still caught up in individuality, but the tide is turning. You find yourself turning around to gaze back at your Source, to contemplate your Oneness. The action of turning around has become a source of nurturance, a source of peace for some of you, and you still return to your individual perspective: your career, your loves, your family, your creativity.

When you take your place as God, active and intent on creatively participating in the evolution of creation, then you become whole. You transcend your humanness and become Divine. You enter into the transcendent mind. There you become a force of nature, dynamic and purposeful. You become an exquisitely Soulful being. Your awareness of your Soul's curriculum allows you to sit in your power. This awareness transforms the consciousness of your species and your planet.

You as God, dreaming yourself, coming to greater awareness that you are God, affects the evolution of all consciousness.

— *Solano*

It has taken several years to write this book. The lengthy process was primarily because I wanted to make sure everything in these pages resonated deeply for me as truth.

I urge you to take all this material and gauge it against your own deep knowing of what truth is for you. Embrace what moves you, what helps you feel more connected to your Soul. Above all else, I've learned through my relationship with the benevolent teacher that each of us has our own lens through which to experience the Divine. Be true to your lens. Hold everything up against your own innate wisdom. Doing so is the only way for you to partner fully with your Soul on your journey.

ABOUT THE AUTHOR

Photo: David Rothmiller

LD THOMPSON was born in Indiana and educated at Indiana University and Alaska Pacific University. In his twenties, the appearance of a mystical stranger dramatically signaled the beginning of a profound spiritual journey. As a result, he dedicated his life to deepening the transformation that he experienced in that meeting, and to integrating the knowledge and the wisdom imparted. LD travels the globe working with individuals, groups, and corporations in the US, Australia, Japan, Germany, and England, as a teacher, advisor and counselor. He advises individuals and corporations alike.

LD's body of work includes a large catalog of recorded programs on a wide array of topics and two meditation CDs: *Coming Home* and *There is an Ocean*. Currently he reaches a worldwide audience in monthly teleconferences that are coordinated through his website (ldthompson.com). In addition to his work as a teacher and counselor, LD is an award-winning documentary filmmaker and video producer. He serves as a Member of the Board of Higher Ground for Humanity.

For a schedule of events, teleconferences,
retreats, CDs, meditations and
personal sessions given by LD Thompson
please visit:

www.ldthompson.com

To book LD Thompson for appearances
please contact:

confluenceonline@gmail.com
Telephone: (310)281-9896

ACKNOWLEDGEMENTS

It is with humble gratitude that I acknowledge those who encouraged and refined, questioned, and guided me in writing this book.

First, I am grateful to all the people who, by making the commitments and engaging the work presented in seminars around the world, have been an incredible support and inspiration in my life.

Along the way, many have promoted and hosted the seminars. Their support has been instrumental in the writing of this book — Robin and Michael Mastro, Camille and Peter Stranger, Sabrina Fox, and Sheila Kenny.

I wish to thank Jayne and Darrel Kays for their dedication to the material. Tinker Lindsay and Valerie Sensabaugh and Annalisa Zox-Weaver for their precision editing and insightful questions; Lenedra

Carroll for her vision of what could be; Thomas Sharkey for never doubting that it would get done.

And Michael Wiese, whose involvement took the book to another level.

Especially, I wish to acknowledge David Rothmiller for being there tirelessly in every aspect of the book from conception and substance to syntax and design. Your creativity is inspiring and I am eternally grateful.

Thank you all from the furthest reaches of my Soul.

And, of course, Solano, without whose wisdom this book would not exist.

an imprint of MICHAEL WIESE PRODUCTIONS

DIVINE
ARTS

DIVINE ARTS sprang to life fully formed as an intention to bring spiritual practice into daily living. Human beings are far more than the one-dimensional creatures perceived by most of humanity and held static in consensus reality. There is a deep and vast body of knowledge – both ancient and emerging – that informs and gives us the understanding, through direct experience, that we are magnificent creatures occupying many dimensions with untold powers and connectedness to all that is. Divine Arts books and films explore these realms, powers and teachings through inspiring, informative and empowering works by pioneers, artists and great teachers from all the wisdom traditions.

We invite your participation and look forward to learning how we may better serve you.

Onward and upward,

Michael Wiese
Publisher/Filmmaker

DivineArtsMedia.com